Cane Toads
and Other Rogue Species

a participant° guide
MEDIA

CANE TOADS

AND OTHER ROGUE SPECIES

Edited by Karl Weber

PUBLICAFFAIRS

New York

Published in the United States by PublicAffairs™,
a member of the Perseus Books Group.

Printed in the United States of America.

PublicAffairs books are available at special discounts for bulk purchases in the U.S.
by corporations, institutions, and other organizations. For more information, please
contact the Special Markets Department at the Perseus Books Group, 2300 Chestnut
Street, Suite 200, Philadelphia, PA 19103, call (800) 810–4145, ext. 5000, or e-mail
special.markets@perseusbooks.com.

Text set in 12-point Minion

Library of Congress Cataloging-in-Publication Data

Cane toads and other rogue species / edited by Karl Weber—1st ed.
     p. cm.
 Includes bibliographical references and index.
 ISBN 978-1-58648–706–5 (pbk.)
 1. Introduced organisms. I. Weber, Karl, 1953–
 QH353.C36 2010
 578.6'2—dc22
                    2010009887

First Edition

10 9 8 7 6 5 4 3 2 1

CONTENTS

PREFACE

There really is nothing quite like a Mark Lewis movie. I suppose if one had to describe it in a single phrase, one would have to call it a "nature documentary," but even to utter those words is to realize how hopelessly inadequate they are at suggesting the odd, lovable blend of deadpan comedy, gentle social satire, and subtly parodic genre play that characterizes a film like Lewis's legendary *Cane Toads*.

Yet at the same time, Lewis's work has much of the appeal—and sheer educational impact—of the traditional nature movie. When you watch *Cane Toads*, or its 2010 sequel *Cane Toads: The Conquest*, you do in fact learn an awful lot about one of the world's most unusual, tenacious, repulsive, yet somehow endearing creatures and its remarkable, and remarkably complex, relationship with the Australian people who have become its unwilling hosts and, some would say, victims. Practically every scene will have you gasping "I didn't know *that*!" even as you are marveling at the technical cleverness of Lewis's film-making technique and the sly humor that infuses it all.

I could go on trying to describe the experience of watching a Mark Lewis picture, but I think I will stop here and simply insist that, if you haven't already had the pleasure of watching *Cane Toads*, you remedy that failure as quickly as possible. Until you do, you can't imagine what you have been missing.

And as you watch the believe-it-or-not story of the cane toad's slow conquest of northern Australia (and the multifarious, often hilarious reactions of the millions of Aussies it encounters), you will gradually come to recognize that this is also a movie about one of the most serious environmental issues of our time—the problem of invasive species and their impact on biological diversity.

In a vague way, we all know that, over the past hundreds and thousands of years, plant and animal species have migrated and spread from their ancestral origins into new habitats elsewhere on the planet. We learn in school about how the Europeans brought the horse to the New World, and perhaps we've picked up some scraps of knowledge about how our favorite foodstuffs have roamed the Earth, often becoming staples in countries quite distant from where they originated (as the potato did in Ireland, or the tomato in Italy). These kinds of transplantations seem colorful and quite benign.

But there's a far more complex, and troubling, side to the story of species migration—one that the tale of the cane toad embodies and that the book in your hand explores in depth. It's a story of human interference with nature—usually well-intentioned but often ignorant, heavy-handed, inadvertent, and blundering, producing unexpected consequences and increasingly threatening the amazing heterogeneity of environments that makes our world so endlessly beautiful and fascinating.

It's about diseases of plants, animals, and humans being carelessly spread from one continent to another by travelers and traders, wreaking havoc among populations that evolution hasn't prepared to cope with them.

It's about pests like the Asian long-horned beetle and the zebra mussel taking over entire ecosystems, ravaging native species, and causing billions of dollars of economic loss.

It's about species like the Burmese python establishing a foothold in environments, such as Florida, that have never known their kind, and threatening destruction to unique endangered competitors for resources like the alligator and panther.

It's about exotic pets being abandoned in foreign habitats, or "set free" by well-meaning but misguided owners, only to end up suffering needless deaths or—perhaps worse—causing the deaths of countless other creatures.

And if allowed to play out to its logical conclusion, species migration may lead to the ecological disaster of a world transformed into what nature writer David Quammen eloquently describes as a "planet of weeds"—a single ecosystem dominated by a handful of ultra-hardy species, in which the wonderful, mind-boggling diversity of the Earth's historic habitats is lost forever.

Biological invasions by creatures traveling from one environment into another are nothing new, of course. There are few impassable boundaries in the natural world; even great mountain ranges, vast deserts, and trackless oceans can be, and have been, crossed by handfuls of adventurous plants and animals—and it takes only a handful to create a colony from which, in time, a population of millions may spring.

But in the modern era—an era of global trade and tourism, and of the increasing homogenization of environments by economic and political forces—the pace at which the planet's inherited species are intermingling has accelerated dramatically, with results no one can predict.

There's no simple solution to this problem. It wouldn't be possible to divide the world into self-contained quarantine zones even if we wanted to try. But in the coming decades, unless the people of the world—themselves the ultimate "invasive species"—learn to take more seriously the implications of their global wanderlust and its biological impacts, we and our children will suffer the unforeseeable results.

The purpose of this book is to serve as a guide to the important, intriguing, and disturbing issue of rogue species. Authored by many of the world's leading experts on invasive species, it has been designed for the lay reader, with the goal of making the entire phenomenon—its causes and consequences—as vivid and understandable as possible. In its pages, you'll discover the stories of many of the world's most amazing creatures—and you'll also learn some of the specific steps we can take, both as individuals and as the collective stewards of Planet Earth, to help protect the global diversity and beauty of nature that we all cherish.

In the end, the journey that begins with *Cane Toads* will take you around the world—and finally back to your own home town, which is where the task of preserving the planet and all the marvelous creatures in it must begin.

Karl Weber
Irvington, New York

PART I

THE CANE TOAD SAGA

The Toad's Tale

A True Fable of Science and Society

Nigel D. Turvey

What drives otherwise pleasant and reasonable people to create environmental havoc? Who were the farmers, politicians, and professional scientists who released such a toxic pest as the cane toad into Australia? Were they alone? What were they thinking? Why did it seem such a good idea at the time?

At the core of these questions is the need to understand such people in their own habitats and their own eras; to understand the influences on them, their backgrounds, their upbringing; to understand their hopes and fears, their thoughts. These were trusted pillars of the community who allowed a few cane toads to be released into an unsuspecting environment. Their ordinary actions had extraordinary impacts.

Such questions drive Nigel Turvey's research and his writings on environmental issues—a unique combination of history and science.

Nigel has roamed the landscapes of Australia and Asia since graduating as an environmental scientist more than thirty-five years ago. As an educator, scientist, and businessman, he worked in the forests of Australia and the rainforests and grasslands of Southeast Asia. He is now working with forest communities, governments, and the timber industry to protect remaining rainforest habitats in Indonesia.

Nigel and his wife, Monica, currently live in the Northern Territory, Australia. Cane toads have just recently arrived there after spending seventy-five years hopping across the top of northern Australia.

In "The Toad's Tale," Turvey explains the amazing history behind the saga of the cane toad—a tale of human folly, hubris, and good intentions gone wrong that offers lessons for all of us.

Seventy-four years after their release in north Queensland, cane toads have covered more than 2,400 kilometers across tropical Australia; the "toad slick" has now reached the far west of the continent.

How did this remarkable expansion happen? Who were the people who triggered it? What could they have been thinking? I wanted to understand more about these people and the times they lived in, and I got lucky. The archive staff in BSES Limited—the successor to the Queensland government's Bureau of Sugar Experiment Stations (BSES), now owned by Australian sugar cane growers and millers—discovered some ancient and rusted files that had survived the Brisbane floods of 1974. Thanks to diligent public service record keeping, and the permission of BSES, I found the chain of events I was looking for.

Water-stained documents in faded musty manila folders revealed the story behind the release of cane toads in Queensland in 1935. It is a tale of biological control gone wrong. But what further emerged was that their release was endorsed by leading international and Australian scientists, stridently supported by the sugar industry, promoted by the premier of Queensland, and even supported by the prime minister of Australia. In short, many prominent people thought that the introduction of cane toads into Queensland's sugar cane fields was a good idea.

For almost three hundred years, the cane toad's tale has been written in the margins of colonial expansion and the sugar trade. In 1735 Carolus Linnaeus, the father of the systematic classification used universally by scientists, met a wealthy collector of natural curiosities, Albertus Seba, who had in his collection in Amsterdam a giant toad purchased from a sailor who brought it from Suriname; it was a by-product of the Dutch trade in slaves, sugar, coffee, and the booty of piracy. Linnaeus included it in his *Systema Naturae* as *Rana marina*; it was later reclassified *Bufo marinus*—

the marine toad. But Linnaeus did not have much regard for toads and their ilk; he reasoned that their "horrible cold bodies, filthy colour . . . fierce faces, ponderous features . . . raucous calls, squalid habitats, and dreadful venom" accounted for why "the Creator had not made many of them."[1]

But the toad—variously called aguaquaquan, sapo grande, marine toad, giant American toad, great Mexican toad, South American toad, Central American toad, Suriname toad, Queensland toad, and, eventually, cane toad—did serve a practical purpose. In the early nineteenth century, the toad was taken from its home in Central and South America to the sugar plantations of the Caribbean to catch insect pests, and rats as well,[2] because it eats whatever comes within range, thus applying an inbuilt logic: If it's big, avoid it; if it's small, eat it; if it's in between, mate with it—scarper, scoff, or screw.

Pest problems in Queensland's new cane fields in the late nineteenth century were much like those in the Caribbean sugar plantations: White grubs, the larvae of local species of greyback canegrubs (sometimes called witchetty grubs), were attacking the roots of sugar cane in preference to tough old native grasses. And the Caribbean experience was so widely known that when Albert Koebele—a disciple of Charles Valentine Riley, the father of biological control—visited Australia in 1888, he declared, "Without doubt the presence of toads . . . would have a remarkable effect in diminishing the number of these [greyback canegrubs] as well as many other injurious insects."[3] But no one followed his advice at the time.

In 1898, after a brief war with Spain, the United States flexed its newfound colonial muscles to take control of Cuba, Puerto Rico, the Philippines, and Guam and annexed Hawaii in the same year. Louisiana's sugar planters were handed a wealth of new territories—and the pests to go with them. Sugar linked America's new lands with Australia; James Chataway, a Mackay sugar planter, was the Queensland correspondent for the newspaper *The Louisiana Planter and Sugar Manufacturer* and, later, as minister for Agriculture and Stock, he brought Walter Maxwell from Hawaii, formerly of Louisiana, to evaluate the state of the sugar industry of Queensland.[4] In December 1900 the Bureau of Sugar Experiment Stations was established under the Queensland Department of Agriculture and Stock, with Walter Maxwell as director employing a succession of American scientists, as well as locals, to solve the sugar industry's problems.

The U.S. Department of Agriculture trained staff to deal with the troubles of emerging agriculture in the new lands. White grubs became so widespread in Puerto Rico that in the early 1920s the Agriculture Experiment Stations on the island imported cane toads from Jamaica and Barbados.[5] Within ten years of their introduction, toads were everywhere and white grubs had all but vanished.[6] But was this entirely the work of the toads? Raquel Dexter, teaching in the biology department of the University of Puerto Rico, devised an experiment to prove a link between the abundance of cane toads and the decline in populations of white grubs. She cut open the stomachs of 301 toads and found that 51 percent of the insects in the toads' stomachs were "injurious to agriculture," 42 percent were "neutral species," and 7 percent were "beneficial" insects.[7] Here was the proof!

In 1932 the members of the International Society of Sugar Cane Technologists gathered for their Fourth Congress in San Juan, Puerto Rico, where Dexter praised the "amphibian immigrant which is doing its full share of benefit to our sugar industry and to which this International Congress should pay a tribute of gratitude."[8]

Queenslander and plant pathologist Arthur Bell represented BSES at the Congress, but he did not hear Dexter's talk because he was busy delivering his own paper in a concurrent session—

the curse of conferences even then. But Cyril Pemberton, entomologist for the Hawaiian Sugar Planters' Association, chaired
Dexter's session. Pemberton was so taken with the "proof" she
presented that he purchased two suitcases and stuffed them with
wood shavings and 152 toads before he sailed for New York,
then took a train to San Francisco and a steamer across the Pacific to release the toads in their new home in Hawaii (149 had
survived).[9]

This was the Great Leap Forward for the cane toad. The 1932
voyage of two suitcases full of toads from the Caribbean Sea to
the middle of the Pacific Ocean was the greatest geographical
leap that *Bufo marinus* had made, and survived to breed, in 40
million years. And thanks to Cyril Pemberton's enthusiasm, Hawaii became the epicenter of the toad's radiation into the islands
of the Pacific.

This is where Australia's problems began—with the myth of
scientific proof. Raquel Dexter's experiment revealed only what
the toads had eaten for their last meals and what their organs were
slow to digest; it proved nothing at all about the dynamics of populations of toads and white grubs. She should have asked whether
the toads' ability to eat anything that wandered close had any effect on populations of female beetles, or on the overall number
of eggs laid, or on the number of beetle eggs turning into white
grubs in cane fields. And what impact did changes in climate, varieties of cane, cultivation techniques, irrigation, and the use of
fertilizers have on populations of white grub in cane fields in the
decade since the introduction of the toad? All of these questions
went unasked, and unanswered.

But the real conundrum is that Pemberton, a senior scientist in
a respected institution, accepted Dexter's conclusions as proof and
with such gusto that he populated Pacific islands with toads. In
Puerto Rico today, according to Dr. David Jenkins, entomologist

in the USDA Mayaguez Research Station, white grubs are back as a pest and the toads are as abundant as ever.[10]

Interest in the toad in Australia was slow to build. In a letter written in September 1933 to his staff at Meringa in north Queensland, Arthur Bell asked whether they thought the toad would help control greyback canegrubs. Reg Mungomery, assistant entomologist, replied to his boss that he did not think toads would be much use because adult female beetles were vulnerable for less than an hour after emerging from the soil before they flew to trees to feed, and the common green frog was already known to eat them with little overall impact on populations.[11] There was no hurrah for the toad at Meringa.

The giant toad was ugly, but in 1933 so was the control of white grubs: soil fumigating with carbon bisulphide or paradichlorobenzene, drilling of white arsenic (arsenic trioxide) into the soil, or dusting with Paris Green (copper acetoarsenate).[12] By contrast, biological control was much less unpleasant and was in vogue in Queensland in the 1930s because Australian ladybird beetles—called vedalia beetles—had successfully been used to control cottony cushion scale infestations in the Californian citrus industry.[13] Queensland scientists had also introduced the moth *Cactoblastis cactorum* from Argentina to control another introduced pest, the prickly-pear cactus. Methods of eradicating prickly pear were vile and ineffective, including arsenic pentoxide, sulphuric acid, and arsenous chloride sprayed by men on horseback.[14] The Commonwealth Prickly Pear Board had tried around 150 different species of insects to control the cactus pest with little success until larvae of the moth proved effective. By 1928, the moth had eradicated the cactus in Queensland, and Reg Mungomery was on the team that made it happen.

The Cactoblastis moth was as spectacularly successful in Queensland as the vedalia beetle was in California, and these well-publicized successes set the scene for the acceptance of biological control in agriculture around the world.

The 1934 season was a good one for greyback canegrubs in Queensland—a bad one for cane growers—and BSES was expected to solve the problem.[15] By the start of 1935, Reg Mungomery had completely changed his mind about the toad. Having read Raquel Dexter's paper and reports of the toad in the West Indies, he wrote to Arthur Bell to say that he now thought the toad would be beneficial in terms of eating not only adult beetles but also weevils, borers, caterpillars, and rats.[16] William Kerr, director of BSES, began arrangements to send Reg Mungomery to Hawaii to collect a colony of giant toads.

In March 1935, Dr. John Cumpston, the Commonwealth director-general of Health, approved the toads' importation.[17] It was an unremarkable event. At the time, the Commonwealth's Quarantine Act, rather than being concerned with importation of pests, was designed to prevent epidemics of influenza and plague in humans and to control the importation of diseased plants and animals.[18]

Mungomery sailed for Hawaii in April 1935 and returned to Sydney on the Matson Line's *Mariposa* in the middle of June 1935, travelling cabin class—the equivalent of business-class travel today—with 102 toads. After breeding them in Meringa, he released 2,400 toads into the Little Mulgrave River and at other sites around Gordonvale in northern Queensland on August 19, 1935.[19] It was just one week before the start of the Fifth Congress of the International Society of Sugar Cane Technologists, hosted in Brisbane by BSES—the successor to the Puerto Rico Congress of three years earlier.

At the Congress, the chief advocate of the toad—Cyril Pemberton from Hawaii—was on hand when Mungomery reported the successful captive breeding of the toad and its release. Congress delegates later viewed the toads at Meringa, where the Queensland minister for Agriculture and Stock, Frank Bulcock, opened the research station.[20] But after the Congress on November 8, 1935, William Kerr, director of BSES, received a bombshell—a telegram from Dr. Cumpston of the Commonwealth Department of Health that prohibited further releases of the toad. The post-Congress euphoria evaporated.

The BSES files reveal the chain of events that led to the ban and the flurry of activity that followed. At the close of the Congress, Pemberton had gone to Sydney to board his ship home to Hawaii, and with some time to spare he had caught up with a colleague, Walter Froggatt, a retired New South Wales government entomologist and then president of the Naturalists' Society of New South Wales. Froggatt was dismayed over Pemberton's news of the introduction of the toad to Queensland and immediately lobbied the Commonwealth government to ban further releases of toads. He warned that "[t]his giant toad, immune from enemies, omnivorous in its habits, and breeding all year round, may become as great a pest as the rabbit or cactus."[21]

Sir David Rivett, chief executive officer of the Council for Scientific and Industrial Research (CSIR)—the forerunner of CSIRO—was brought into the debate, but he supported BSES, saying, "I am very glad to know that Mr C. E. Pemberton is prepared to defend the wisdom of the importation despite the decidedly pessimistic forecast of the New South Wales entomologist."[22] But his support was self-serving, because CSIR was working on the release of the European toad, *Bufo vulgaris*, to control pests in pastures. There was additional support for the toad from Robert Veitch, the chief entomologist of Queensland, as well as representation in person from Arthur Bell in Canberra, but Dr. Cumpston was unmoved.[23]

It was time for the sugar industry to flex its considerable electoral muscles. The director of BSES, William Kerr, wrote to the

Australian Sugar Producers' Association and the Queensland Cane Growers' Council announcing the ban. The Council's secretary, Bill Doherty, immediately telegraphed his members asking for "strong agitation against Federal authorities."[24] Kerr also briefed his minister, Frank Bulcock, who in turn sent a glowing recommendation of the toad to the premier of Queensland, William Forgan Smith, suggesting he make representations to the prime minister.[25] Forgan Smith was a former minister for Agriculture and Stock and represented the sugar seat of Mackay; he had championed the sugar industry throughout the Depression and had recently addressed international delegates at the Sugar Technologists' Congress.[26]

But here the paper trail ended; BSES had no need to see the correspondence between the premier and the prime minister, and I had to track the next letter through the Queensland State Archives. And there it was. On December 2, 1935, Forgan Smith sent the prime minister, Joseph Lyons, an almost verbatim version of Bulcock's letter—a copy of the original letter from William Kerr—requesting that the ban be lifted.[27] The very next day, Dr. Cumpston telegraphed the Queensland undersecretary for Agriculture and Stock to partially lift the ban, and the prime minister added later that "no objection would be raised against the release of toads in those areas in which liberations have already been made"—the Cairns, Gordonvale, and Innisfail region.[28]

Here was the smoking gun; support for the toad went right to the top, and the sugar lobby was strong enough that Joseph Lyons was able to overrule his head of the Department of Health—in an instant.

An unhappy Dr. Cumpston wrote to the Queensland undersecretary to say, "It is recognised, of course, that your Government is prepared to accept its share of responsibility for the action which is now being taken."[29] BSES still wanted the ban lifted completely because cane growers were now calling for their allocation of toadlets, but first it had to satisfy a snubbed and unhappy Dr. Cumpston.

Walter Froggatt's criticisms of the toad became public in January 1936, when his article was published in *The Australian Naturalist*.[30] As a former government entomologist, Froggatt had been responsible for knocking on the head other crazy proposals for biological control, including a plan to use red meat-ants from South Africa to destroy baby rabbits in their burrows; a scheme to use ferrets, stoats, weasels, and the mongoose to exterminate rabbits; and an inspired suggestion to import vultures from Texas to control blowflies.[31] About the toads he wrote: "There is no limit to their westward range, and [they] . . . will probably adapt themselves to our mountain ranges, and even reach the river banks and swamp lands of the interior."[32]

There in the BSES files, among the bland carbon copies of official correspondence, is a letter from Walter Froggatt to Arthur Bell, handwritten on the letterhead of the Naturalists' Society of New South Wales and graced with its gum leaf emblem. With a career of experience behind him and summoning as much passion as possible in the two dimensions of the page and the protocol of the medium, Walter Froggatt had written: "No organisation, or even a single state of the Commonwealth has the right to independently introduce such a possible menace to the continent as *Bufo marinus*."[33]

In July 1936, the Queensland undersecretary for Agriculture and Stock collated the BSES defense of the toad for the benefit of Dr. Cumpston. It included a detailed critique of Froggatt's article, a letter from Cyril Pemberton supporting the "beneficial and innocuous creature," a review of literature, and a further character reference for the toad from Hawaii.[34] In August 1936, Arthur Bell, perpetuating the charade of science, sent Dr. Cumpston yet another copy of Raquel Dexter's paper and a repeat of her experiment on toads by the staff of BSES (except that, inexplicably, in this case they examined the toads' excreta for evidence of their last meals).[35]

Two studies of the toads' diet seemed to convince Dr. Cumpston. There was no request for additional ecological studies; he lifted the ban on the wider release of the toad in September 1936.[36] But the damage had been done a year earlier when the first toads had been released. With a female toad capable of spawning around thirty thousand eggs at a sitting, there was no hope of getting those tadpoles back in the jar.

The BSES team at Meringa continued to breed and distribute thousands of cane toads around the sugar-growing areas of Queensland for at least another three years.

Reg Mungomery's initial assessment was correct—cane toads did not control white grubs. And Walter Froggatt proved to be a prescient critic—cane toads would reach far beyond the Kakadu wetlands. The toad's subsequent colonization of a 4,000-kilometer band of tropical and subtropical Australia was the greatest mass migration in its globe-trotting history.

Today, it is easy to point a derisory finger at the individuals involved and the three critical errors they made. First, their assumption that the toad would control greyback canegrubs was wrong because the feeding habits of the toad did not coincide with the swarming habits of the adult beetles. Second, the interpretation of Raquel Dexter's experiment as proving the link between the feeding habits of the toad and a decline in populations of white grubs was fundamentally flawed. And third, there was no recognition of the wisdom of Walter Froggatt's warning of the ecological impact of a toxic amphibian on the fauna of subtropical and tropical Australia.

The premise was bad, the assumption flawed, and the execution reckless.

Who was to blame? Did the sugar industry and the politicians pressure the scientists into precipitate action? Did the scientists foist their idea on an industry and a government that trusted them? Or did they work together to support an idea that they all believed would be the savior of the sugar industry? Bits of evidence can support each case. But blame is pointless—there is no recourse.

Instead, we need to learn what went wrong so as to avoid a repeat performance. There appears to have been no failure to follow quarantine procedures at the time; we can fault the procedures themselves, but later amendments to the Quarantine Act closed the gaping holes. The problem seems to have originated with the blinkered members of the chain of command who believed that what they were doing would help the sugar industry. It is a problem that lies within the people and the mindset of the times.

Think back to 1935. The Sugar Technologists' Congress had met in Brisbane under what its president called "a continuance of the acute economic depression which has enveloped the entire world."[37] At the same time, President Franklin D. Roosevelt was implementing his New Deal to lift America out of economic depression, and the chancellor of Germany, Adolf Hitler, was flouting the Versailles Treaty and stirring up talk of war. A mindset of war also prevailed in Australia: Sugar regulations had given financial encouragement for white labor to populate tropical Australia with what sugar growers called "a defensive garrison" against a "temptation to Asiatic invasion,"[38] and scientists believed they were engaged on behalf of mankind in "continuous warfare upon the insects" that attacked the cane.[39] This was the milieu of William Kerr, Arthur Bell, and Reg Mungomery of BSES; Bill Doherty of the Queensland Cane Growers' Council; Robert Veitch, Queensland's chief entomologist; Sir David Rivett, the head of CSIR; John Cumpston, the director-general of Health; William Forgan

Smith, the premier of Queensland; and Joseph Lyons, the prime minister of Australia. They were men of their times, not evil-doers bent on populating Australia with a toxic pest.

Now ask: If you were one of them, what would be your response to a carping critic who in 1935 wanted to know "What effect will releasing tadpoles in the Little Mulgrave River in Queensland have on the ecology of the Kimberley region on the other side of Australia?"

Clearly, people at all levels of the decision to import the toad should have asked and answered that very question—but they didn't.

Is science the culprit? The toad was championed by qualified scientists, some eminent in their fields, but scientists are not an homogeneous breed. The science philosopher Sir Peter Medawar described them well: "Among scientists are collectors, classifiers, and compulsive tidiers-up; many are detectives by temperament and many are explorers; some are artists and other artisans." As Medawar went on to say, scientists tell stories, "stories which might be about real life, but which have to be tested very scrupulously to find out if indeed they are so."[40]

Some scientists will argue that the "scientific method" of hypothesis and testing was not applied in the case of the cane toad, but that is how science is *reported*, not necessarily how it is *done*; science is rather more haphazard, and the wastelands of scientific endeavor are dotted with blooms of serendipity. It is easy to say that by current standards the science behind the introduction of the toad was poor, but it should be judged by the standards of 1935—not by those of today. What is more worrying is that the number of qualified scientists supporting the toad's introduction indicates that the standard of scientific evidence applied in this case must have passed as acceptable for the times.

We may be appalled by what passed as acceptable science in 1935, but in seventy-five years our descendants will likely be appalled by many of *our* actions—our profligate use of energy and water, the gross imbalance of our carbon economy, the naïveté of our genetic manipulation. But will they also be appalled by what we think of as good things that we have done? Just as in 1935, each generation of researchers believes it is at the forefront of science, but the front keeps moving and researchers are left in its wake. And in the end, good science will deliver a good scientific outcome—but it will not guarantee a benign one.

Could a mistake like the cane toad fiasco happen again today? Could another alien organism, championed by respected scientists, government departments, and politicians, be released in Australia? Consider the 1935 proposal in the light of modern criteria for research funding, and imagine the PowerPoint presentation:

THE CANE TOAD

- builds on successes in biological control.
- replaces toxic pesticides.
- is supported by a published scientific paper.
- has international scientific peer review.
- is endorsed by Australia's leading science body.
- is championed by the industry.
- is promoted by the Queensland government and its premier.
- is approved for use by the Commonwealth government.
- has personal endorsement from the prime minister.

It is a dead-set winner—straight to the top of the funding list. Yes, it could happen again.

The toad was championed in Australia by a herd of supporters including scientists, industry people, and government officials. But in every herd there are people like Walter Froggatt who can see farther than the rest, who can see the precipice, yet whose voices are lost in the thunder of hooves. In a stampede, the collective ego is blind, the herd instinct is contagious, and naysayers get trampled. But that is just the time when we must turn the mob, settle the herd, and ask questions that could have them all grazing quietly once more. We must ask for scrupulous testing of the stories that scientists tell and question assumptions about the ecological impacts—in seventy-five years or more—of the organisms they are releasing now.

Sadly, until today's scientists can remedy the catastrophe of their predecessors' making, much of the fauna of the Top End of Australia will have to live or die by the toad.

The Making—and the Meaning—
of *Cane Toads: The Conquest*

MARK LEWIS

Mark Lewis heads Radio Pictures Inc., an independent film production company. Born in Sydney, Australia, he graduated with a Bachelor's in economics from Sydney University and later attended the Australian Film and Television School, graduating in direction.

His documentary credits include *Cane Toads*, *The Wonderful World of Dogs*, and *RAT*. His films have earned numerous awards and have been screened at the world's leading film festivals. His film *The Natural History of the Chicken* was screened in competition at Sundance and was named by the *New York Times* as one of the top ten television programs for 2001. Mark Lewis won two Emmys for the film, one for Outstanding Science Program and the other for Outstanding Direction.

With Barry Humphries and David Mitchell, Lewis recently wrote the screenplay adaptation of *My Gorgeous Life*, a bio-pic of one of the world's greatest actresses, Dame Edna Everage. In 2009, Lewis finished delivering four one-hour prime-time programs for a PBS and ABC series titled *The Pursuit of Excellence*.

Among the critical raves Lewis has received, his favorites include "He has brought a deadpan sensibility and a vibrantly quirky visual style to the nature documentary" (Julie Salamon, *New York Times*) and "His excellent, funny films end up being less about animals than about humans" (*New Yorker*).

In these pages, Lewis explains the story behind his remarkable cane toad movies as well as the broader motivations that have shaped the career of one of today's most unusual film makers.

Perhaps I should begin by addressing the obvious question— Why make a movie about cane toads? It's a question that's especially poignant for me, since I now find myself in the unique position of having made *two* movies about the same subject. As a result, I've been living with cane toads (figuratively and sometimes literally) for the better part of the past twenty-five years. Based on the reputation I've developed, you'd almost think I'd adopted "Cane Toad" as my middle name—and it's an extraordinarily difficult one to shake off.

My first encounter with the cane toad came when I was just nineteen or twenty years old. I was then, and remain today, an avid motorcyclist, and I was motorcycling into Queensland from New South Wales. One night it was raining as I came around a bend in a highway, and there before me I was suddenly confronted with hundreds, no, thousands of cane toads covering the road. It was an extraordinary sight, one that many other people have come to experience and one that has stuck with me to this day.

Years later when I was a radio journalist at the Australian Broadcasting Corporation (ABC) I saw a newspaper paragraph about the cane toads and their extraordinary march toward the south. It struck me as an odd and weirdly fascinating story, and I began clipping articles about these persistent, tough little animals. Over the years I became fascinated by the inconsistent stories, folk lore, and myths that I encountered about the cane toad.

The more I learned, the weirder it got. One day, I read how the Queensland police had busted a bunch of "hippies" for "smoking cane toads." Then another day, I read about an elderly lady who decided she adored cane toads and had begun adopting them as pets. And the day after that, I read about a town that had organized a militia to hunt the things down and eradicate them. It was just an array of bizarre stories, spanning the worlds of science and pop culture, and eventually I was intrigued.

And I also discovered that, although the cane toad story was very Australian and seemingly parochial, it had enormous universal implications—as I'll discuss a little later.

I stumbled into movie making almost by accident. My academic background had been in economics and politics. After university, I spent three years bumming my way around the world, finding myself gravitating toward creative people and experimenting with various ways of making a living. For example, I worked with the aerialist Philippe Petit on his daring (and illegal) feat of walking on a tightrope between the Twin Towers in New York. Years later, the Oscar-winning film *Man on Wire* documented this adventure.

When I returned to Australia, I joined the ABC as a radio journalist doing commentary on public interest topics. After a year and a half I was selected for the Australian film school and, following that, spent several years as a location sound mixer working on all kinds of films, probably the best-known being *The Coca-Cola Kid*.

Eventually, I got frustrated with that, because, like many technicians, I believed I could do a better job than the director! And so I put together a proposal to do a movie about this weird, amazing story I'd been following—the tale of the cane toad. I got funding from a government entity called Film Australia, which was working to promote and strengthen the national film industry. And that allowed me to go out and make my first movie. So in a very real sense, I owe my career to cane toads. No wonder I'm partial to them.

In the years since 1988, when the first *Cane Toads* was released, I've made various movies about animals. As the critics have kindly informed me—and in this case I think they happen to be quite right—my pictures are not so much about their animal subjects (whether cane toads, chickens, or rats) as about the relationship between animals and human beings. All the animals I find interesting are ones that are somehow entwined with humans.

This makes my films quite different from traditional natural history documentaries, which are often about creatures like lions, elephants, or dolphins. In those pictures, the film makers try to capture the lives of the animals in a kind of pristine, natural state, as if untouched by humans—which is ironic, since the only animals they can ever really get close enough to film are ones that are habituated to the presence of humans in the first place. But judging by the footage you see on screen, there are no people within a hundred miles of the jungle or ocean depths where we see the animals "naturally" cavorting.

In a way, my films are a kind of send-up of those traditional safari movies, which frankly I've always found a bit pretentious. (Or is it portentous? Maybe both.) People tell me I have a cheeky sense of humor, and I suppose my movies are my way of expressing it. I enjoy parodying some of the all-too-familiar clichés found in those pictures—for example, the Mating Scene and the Fearsome-Predator-Captures-His-Prey Scene. As you've no doubt observed, I have fun tweaking the genre with my own tongue-in-cheek versions of those scenes.

For example, cane toad *amplexus*—their mating ritual—was depicted in my first movie with scenes showing a cane toad mating with a scientist's boot or with a dead cane toad lying in the road. (Not exactly the way the film makers at Disney or National Geographic would do it.) And in *Cane Toads: The Conquest* I've depicted *amplexus* as a romantic love vignette, placing the cane toads in a swamp bedecked with flowers. It's quite beautiful and romantic, I think—and true to life, by the way.

In the first *Cane Toads*, I also found myself playing off the conventions of the horror movie—for example, with a shower scene stylistically reminiscent of *Psycho*. That was a result not just of my sense of humor but also of the nature of the media coverage that the cane toad receives. News stories about the cane toad are always couched in terms designed to provoke anxiety if not terror—they talk about *war, alien invasion, the implacable enemy*. Scientists and journalists both gravitate toward this language, I suppose as a way of making their work and their message seem that much more grave and important. And again, I can't help wanting to puncture this sort of pretension when I encounter it. Hence the note of parody some people have spotted in my pictures.

I do this in a gentle way. Some of my strategies are rather subtle, I think. For example, I always try to show scientists in a lab, wearing white jackets. Naturally this serves as a clear signal to the viewer as to who is speaking. But it also puts the scientists firmly in their specific context, which is not necessarily as all-encompassing as they might like to think. Over the years, I've found that laypeople tend to have a much broader grasp of what animals are really like, how they live, and how they interact with humans than the scientists, who tend to have a narrow, specialized perspective based on their particular field of study—the gall bladder, say, or the cane toad's sense of hearing. That's why I like to use the voices of laypeople as much as possible in my movies. They often know so much more than the "experts" who dominate the traditional natural history film.

By the way, scientists seem to like my work despite my gentle tweaking of them. Naturally enough, they appreciate anything that highlights their own work—and when an issue like the cane toad gets onto the front pages of newspapers, it probably makes it easier for them to get government grants in support of their research. So the scientists and I get along quite well, which is a good thing, since I have learned so much from them and worked with them to our mutual benefit over the years.

Nor have I received any complaints about the impact of my films on the global image of Australia. Oddly enough, I don't think the notion of northern Australia as being overrun by millions of huge brown toads has actually hurt our tourism industry a bit. It's funny—when Baz Luhrmann spent something like $130 million making his so-called epic *Australia*, some of the media here were jumping up and down with excitement about the flood of visitors the movie would attract from around the world. But in fact (and it seems quite ironic to me), the movie was set in an extremely hot, fly-ridden dust bowl—the fictitious cattle station of "Faraway Downs"!

By contrast, my cane toad pictures are really a kind of showcase for Australia. In its expansion across the northern half of the country, the cane toad has journeyed from lush rain forests to the desert, and in tracing this epic journey—especially in *Cane Toads: The Conquest*—we've produced something of a travelogue that will introduce people to aspects of Australia they've never seen before.

The vast extent of the march of the cane toads has taken most of the experts by surprise. Twenty-five years ago, when I made the first film, there were all kinds of predictions as to where the cane toad might someday migrate. Those have proven to be woefully over-conservative. Today the animal has expanded much farther west and south than anyone ever imagined possible. So I don't suppose that anyone today can really anticipate where the toad may wind up tomorrow, or the day after that. Some find that alarming, but I find it fascinating and, in a perverse way, inspiring.

It had always been in the back of my mind that a follow-up movie might be a good idea. With the success of the first *Cane Toads*, for years afterward people sent me clippings of every newspaper and magazine article about this creature. I ended up with a vast mass of ephemera about the topic, which made it clear that the story was developing in many new ways that deserved exploration.

It was left to Clark Bunting, a longtime executive at the Discovery Channel, to formally propose the new picture. Clark discovered Steve Irwin (of TV's "Crocodile Hunter" fame), helped create the Animal Planet network, and is now president of the Discovery Channel. He and I have been friends for many years, and now Discovery has partnered with Participant Media to make *Cane Toads: The Conquest* a reality.

I should clarify, to avoid any misconceptions, that *Cane Toads: The Conquest* is not a "remake." All the stories and characters in this film are new. We're revisiting this moving army of toads as it encounters new places and people, creating great acrimony and hostility wherever it travels—and also provoking new responses by people who love employing cane toads in a variety of ways. There are artists who employ road-kill toads in their artwork, others who craft dresses out of toad skins, still others who make toad dioramas out of stuffed toads. My friend Barry Humphreys, known to the world as Dame Edna Everage, has his favorite books bound in cane toad leather. And of course there is the vast realm of cane toad memorabilia and souvenirs—cane toad wallets and shoulder bags and key rings and hats and belt buckles, and what have you. A Gold Coast brewery even came out with Cane Toad Beer. The first movie increased the demand for such items, and perhaps the second will do the same. And I've never collected any royalties, more's the pity!

On a technical level, the new project has been extraordinarily challenging and fun. We shot *Cane Toads: The Conquest* in 3D—in fact, it's the first independent movie shot in 3D in Australia. So we're breaking a number of boundaries technically.

But the first movie, while seemingly simpler in style, was also very innovative. For example, we tried to tell much of the story from the cane toad's point of view, using exceptionally low camera angles—in effect, giving a voice to this animal that couldn't speak for itself yet was at the center of so much controversy. My goal was to create some sympathy for this animal that was so widely reviled.

A second innovation was to present all of the interviewees in what I call "first person." Rather than having the interviewees—the characters, as I call them—speaking to an off-stage interviewer, as you see in traditional documentaries, I wanted to let them speak directly to the audience. So I devised a camera accessory I call a "mirror box," which allows the character to speak straight into the camera lens while looking directly at me, the interviewer, thus creating a subconscious connection between the character and the audience.

Since then, this device or something similar has been used by other film makers, including Errol Morris, the American documentarian, who used it in the movie *Fast, Cheap, and Out of Control.* He called his apparatus an "interrotron," but it's much the same thing as the mirror box.

Finally, Jim Frazier, the cameraman on the first *Cane Toads,* developed a set of lenses that allowed us to get extraordinarily close to the toad and keep it in focus, while also maintaining focus on other objects much deeper in the frame. Later this gave rise to what is called the Panavision/Frazier lens system, which combines deep focus with great breadth of field. *Cane Toads* was one of the first films to employ a version of this technology.

So my first *Cane Toads* was quite innovative for its day—just as *Cane Toads: The Conquest* has proven to be.

●— ●— ●—

John Grierson, often dubbed "the father of the documentary," referred to the art of nonfiction film making as "the creative treatment of actuality." Personally, I hate the term "documentarian." (I think it makes one sound like some sort of librarian.) I prefer the simpler term "film maker." As a maker of nonfiction films, I have a method of preparation that is probably different from what most movie makers employ.

Before I begin shooting film, I create a script and storyboards for many sequences in the picture. This requires an enormous bout of advance research. At one time, I would have begun this process by going on talk shows and placing ads asking for stories related to my topic—the cane toad, for example. The resulting harvest would become the basis for my subsequent research and story development.

Today I don't bother with the advertising process. Instead, I subscribe to the online search service Nexis and use it to do a lot of trolling through newspaper and magazine stories dating back fifteen or twenty years. On a popular topic, this creates a vast database of information. For example, we might have six or seven hundred citations about cane toads every year. I spend months going through those stories and try to develop a sense as to which ones might be unique and relevant for the movie, yielding characters that would be great to film and include.

As we do all this research, we keep editing and refining stories, and eventually we start contacting characters to explore their suitability for the picture and their willingness to participate. We might interview them on the phone so as to begin developing a sense of their narrative, as well as to allow them to get to know us and to trust us.

Ultimately, we pick the most appropriate character—the very best scientist, politician, policeman, farmer, or suburban homeowner—to embody a particular aspect of the story we want to tell. We develop a notebook of content for each of the characters that includes a series of questions we will use to elicit their story. Finally, we schedule a time to film them in an appropriate setting, usually allocating two or three days to be with them, including one full day for interviewing and the rest for capturing the setting and context.

It's an exhaustive process, but I find it absolutely necessary to create the sense of actuality and life that I hope my films convey.

And what about some larger "truth"? Do my films communicate anything more to the viewer than the simple fascination of a strange story vividly depicted on screen?

I'll leave it to individual viewers to determine that. But there's no way to escape the truth that the cane toad saga is an extraordinary tale of a well-intended scientific effort to control an inconvenient pest gone wrong. And it's a story that raises many serious and important questions, which I hope my films evoke.

Personally, I'm sympathetic to the toads, and a bit allergic to some of the alarmist rhetoric that anti–cane toad activists employ. Has the cane toad actually played a significant role in killing off any native Australian species? (As far as I am aware, the answer is no.) Is the environmental damage it creates worse than that created by, say, the donkey (which is another introduced species) or by ill-considered fire management practices? (Again, I think the answer is no.) There's no doubt that the spread of cane toads across half of the Australian continent is a strange phenomenon that the well-meaning individuals who first imported the creatures would never have expected or wanted. But it's far from unique in the annals of human-animal interaction, and we need to think about it in that context.

But I'm not out to proselytize. I'm a film maker, and I'm drawn to subjects I find interesting. And although I would never call myself an "educator," it's true that my films are very "educational." It's wonderful to know how many universities around the world use my films as teaching tools in classes on environmental science or media studies.

It's a great side effect of my film-making method that important issues get raised by my films, although my style is to let my characters raise them for me. So when you watch *Cane Toads: The Conquest*, you may hear one character say, "We're spending $6 million saving the whale. Why not spend that money on killing cane toads?" while another will ask, "Why scapegoat the cane toad when the camel is causing more damage in the Northern Territories than the toad has ever done?" I like the idea of letting characters have their point of view.

As I've already confessed, I'm partial to the cane toad. I hope people who watch my films will understand why. But in any case I'm happy that important issues about the globalization of animals, biodiversity, and the role of science in our society get raised by my films, and I hope they'll stimulate some lively, intelligent discussion about the topics.

PART II

ROGUE SPECIES
AND THE FUTURE OF THE PLANET

The Rogue Species Threat— Why Should We Care?

JEFFREY A. MCNEELY

Jeffrey A. McNeely is senior science advisor at the International Union for the Conservation of Nature (IUCN), the world's oldest and largest global environmental network, with more than a thousand institutional members and ten thousand scientists and other specialists working in biological conservation and dedicated to helping the world find pragmatic solutions to our most pressing environmental and development challenges.

McNeely has worked at the IUCN since 1980. Previously, he spent twelve years in Thailand, Indonesia, and Nepal, conducting research and overseeing practical applications of resource management activities. He has written or edited more than forty books and five hundred popular and technical articles on a wide range of environmental topics, and has served on the editorial board of fourteen international journals. He is currently working to link biodiversity to sustainable agriculture, human health, biotechnology, climate change, energy, and more traditional fields of IUCN interest such as species preservation, protected areas, ecosystems, and economics.

McNeely is a co-founder of the Global Invasive Species Programme and has published extensively on the topic of invasive alien species. He is chairman of the board of Ecoagriculture Partners, president of the Asia Section of the Society for Conservation Biology, a member of the Scientific and Technical Council of the International Risk Governance Council, science patron of Earthwatch Europe, a member of the Board of Trustees of the Foundation for Environmental Conservation, a fellow of the World Academy of Art and Science, a member of the UNEP International

Panel for Sustainable Resource Management, an A. D. White Professor at Large at Cornell University, an adjunct professor at Peking University, and a member of the Order of the Golden Ark.

In "The Rogue Species Threat," McNeely explains, through vivid examples and with a powerful scientific perspective, exactly why the problem of invasive species has become so widespread—and how it is already having an impact on every one of us.

Many of the deadly threats to our natural world are difficult to ignore. Pollution, climate change, habitat loss, and over-consumption make daily headlines and force actions by governments. But one threat slips under the public's radar and often goes unnoticed even by conservation organizations—despite the fact that most experts consider it the second most dangerous hazard currently faced by nature. This subtle peril brings deadly diseases to plants, animals, and people. Its impacts cost billions of dollars in direct damage every year, plus more billions spent to repair the damage.

This menace arrives through a basically benevolent channel— global trade—but its name should be ringing alarm bells around the world: *invasive alien species.*

Invasive aliens are plants, animals, fungi, and micro-organisms that usually play a normal and healthy role in their native ecosystems but can cause havoc when they arrive on foreign shores.

Mind you, these rogue species represent only a small proportion of the species introduced from afar. Most natural guests, whether invited by humans or arriving as party crashers, fit comfortably into the native cast of life—in some cases, even enriching ecosystems.

We humans owe a lot to non-native species. Without them, Russia would have no vodka (since potatoes are an introduced crop), Italy would have no pizza (at least, not topped with tomato sauce), Americans would grow no wheat for their daily bread, and Colombian coffee would be just a fantasy. Indeed, most of the crops that feed most of the planet originated someplace other than where they are grown most productively today. (Rice is the main exception.) Of course, countless native species continue to thrive in their native lands—often with great genetic diversity, as is true of the many varieties of potatoes grown in their ancestral home of Peru. But the entire world has benefited biologically from being able to grow crops that originated elsewhere. Our foods, organic medicines, ornamental plants, and timber harvests have all benefited from this global exchange.

So what's the problem?

For millennia, the natural barriers of oceans, mountains, rivers, and deserts provided the geographic isolation essential for unique species and ecosystems to evolve. However, in just a few hundred years these barriers have been rendered ineffective by new transport technologies and economic imperatives that have combined to help alien species travel vast distances to new habitats and become threats to native ecosystems and human welfare.

Nobody is arguing against improving human welfare through providing greater access to the world's biological resources. But we need to worry about the relatively few non-native species that cause damage to native ecosystems and to human welfare. Thus the Convention on Biological Diversity, in its Article 8(h), calls for parties to the Convention to "prevent the introduction of, control, or eradicate those alien species which threaten ecosystems, habitats or species." Such species are commonly called invasive alien species, and they include only a small fraction of the total number of non-native species that may enter a country. Yet the Millennium Ecosystem Assessment describes invasive species as one of the five leading drivers of ecosystem degradation.[1] Why?

In the next few pages, I'll provide several answers to this question, including economic and ethical issues, with ecosystem productivity, human health, biodiversity, and climate change thrown into the mix.

THE THREAT TO HUMAN HEALTH

The globalization of and growth in the volume of trade and tourism, coupled with the emphasis on free trade, provide more opportunities than ever before for pathogens to be spread accidentally or deliberately. Customs and quarantine practices, developed in an earlier time to guard against human diseases and economic pests, are inadequate safeguards against new threats to human health posed by expanding global trade.

Invasions by humans and other species have historically been important causes of the spread of infectious disease, associated with increases in human population density, interpopulation mobility, intensification of trade, and changes in land use that simplify and disturb ecological systems.

Ancient Athens, Rome, and Constantinople were dealt staggering blows by spectacular new epidemic infections brought in from Middle Eastern and Indian sources by traders and armies. The most severe type of malaria (*Plasmodium falciparum*), for example, is thought to have been introduced from Southwest Asia and northern Africa into Europe via trade and military campaigns.

Rinderpest, an introduced disease of livestock, facilitated the European colonial conquest of Africa at the end of the nineteenth century by weakening the pastoralists. As one colonist observed, "Powerful and warlike as the pastoral tribes are, their pride has been humbled and our progress facilitated by this awful visitation. The advent of the white man had not else been so peaceful."

An alien plant known as *Ambrosia artemisiifolia* first appeared in France in the 1860s, but it expanded explosively during the reconstruction works that followed the end of World War II. It is a threat to human and animal health, provoking skin rashes, respiratory allergies, sinusitis, and conjunctivitis.

In more modern times, the global movement of ballast water by ships has created a long-distance dispersal mechanism for human pathogens and may be an important factor in the worldwide distribution of micro-organisms, as well as in the epidemiology of waterborne diseases affecting plants and animals. In 2000, a team of scientists measured the concentration of the bacteria *Vibrio cholerae*, which cause human epidemic cholera, in the ballast water of vessels arriving at Chesapeake Bay from foreign ports. They found cholera bacteria in plankton samples from all of the ships they tested and concluded that coastal ecosystems are frequently invaded by micro-organisms from ballast water.[2]

Concentrations of bacteria and viruses exceed those reported for other taxonomic groups in ballast water by six to eight orders of magnitude, and the probability of successful invasion increases with the population of the invader. Furthermore, the biology of many micro-organisms may facilitate invasion, combining a high capacity for increased population size, asexual reproduction, and the ability to form resting stages that may remain dormant as the micro-organisms are transported around the world. Such flexibility in life history can broaden the opportunity for successful colonization, allowing rapid population growth when the invaders arrive where suitable environmental conditions welcome their pioneers to establish a beachhead and multiply quickly. And, third, many micro-organisms can tolerate a broad range of environmental conditions such as salinity or temperature, so many sites may provide a warm welcome for colonization. Given the magnitude of ongoing transfer and its potential consequences for ecological and disease processes, large-scale movement of micro-organisms by ships merits special attention.

In August 2007, Italy suffered the first known outbreak of a relative of dengue fever, known as *Chikungunya*, carried by tiger mosquitoes, which have now invaded Europe. Their invasion is at least partly due to the warming trend being experienced by Italy and much of the rest of Europe. The tiger mosquito first arrived in Ravenna, Italy, in 2004, but has since spread across southern Europe into France and Switzerland. Further and more widespread outbreaks of the fever are expected in Europe in the coming years.

Several invasive alien species of mosquitoes are capable of carrying the West Nile virus. These include *Aedes japonicus*, which arrived in the late 1990s and is found in Connecticut, and *Aedes albopictus*, which arrived in used car tires in the early 1980s and is found in northern New Jersey (at least). Both are said to be very efficient vectors of the West Nile virus and to bite during the day.[3] In 2002, more than 3,200 people contracted West Nile virus in the United States; of these, 177 died.

Invasive plants are a human health problem, too. In Tanzania, *Lantana camara* thickets provide breeding grounds for tsetse flies infected with trypanosomes of domestic animals, and children are known to have died after eating its unripe berries. In just two villages in Rwanda, as many as 25 people have recently been confirmed to be suffering from sleeping sickness (trypanosomiasis), which is carried by tsetse flies. The reemergence of sleeping sickness is attributed to the rapid expansion of invasive *Lantana camara*, which harbors the tsetse flies.

THE SPREAD OF DISEASE TO NATIVE SPECIES

Human deaths by West Nile virus are tragic enough, but the bird populations of North America have been devastated by the disease, with fatality rates as high as 90 percent for crows, the species most sensitive to the virus. Birds of prey appear to be dying at ten times their usual number in several states in the United States. More than a hundred species of North American birds are known to be infected by the West Nile virus, but the ubiquitous house sparrow (itself an invasive species) carries the virus without showing symptoms. Endangered species of birds, such as the Florida scrub jay, could become extinct as a result of this invasive species. Europe, too, is affected by a closely related virus, known as Usutu, which has killed thousands of blackbirds in Vienna.[4]

Invasive species may be accompanied by disease organisms that attack their competitors. For example, the decline of red squirrels in Britain that began in 1900 may have been caused by a parapox-virus transmitted from introduced North American grey squirrels in which it is benign.[5]

Thus, many of the ecological impacts of disease and invasives may be highly complex, affecting ecosystems in many ways. As just one example, high mortality of rabbits after the introduction of myxomytosis in the U.K. led to population declines in their predators, including stoats, buzzards, and owls. The impact was also felt indirectly on other species—leading, for instance, to local extinction of the endangered large blue butterfly by reducing grazing pressure on heathlands, which, in turn, removed the habitat for an ant species that assists developing butterfly larvae. Introduced diseases have been implicated in the extirpation of many species and the extinction of Hawaiian birds, reptiles in the Mascarene Islands, Pleistocene megafauna, and others.

Plants are also suffering from invasive pathogens. A new species of tree fungus in the genus *Phytophthora* has caused a disease called sudden oak death, attacking tan oak, coast live oak, and black oak trees in California. The death rate of trees in these three species has accelerated alarmingly due to this fungus, leaving large areas with dead trees that are very prone to fire. Oak trees dominate some 4 million hectares along 2,400 kilometers of the California and Oregon coast, and hundreds of animal species, some of them threatened, depend on the trees.

The chestnut blight fungus (*Cryphonectria parasitica*) had a devastating impact on the temperate deciduous forests of eastern North America. First recorded in New York City in 1904, chestnut blight is thought to have been introduced along with Japanese chestnut trees (*C. crenata*) that were imported as nursery stock. The blight spread at a rate of 30 to 80 kilometers per year, virtually wiping out the American chestnut throughout its range by 1950. The American chestnut (*C. dentate*) was once the dominant and most abundant tree species in the hardwood forests of North America, but it was extirpated through most of its range by the chestnut blight, removing from the ecosystem an important timber and fuel wood tree that provided an abundant and high-quality food resource for people, wildlife, and livestock throughout much of eastern North America. In a desperate last-ditch effort to save the species from extinction, scientists are now using biological control methods involving a virus, hybridization, and backcrossing through the Chinese chestnut (*C. mollissima*), which is resistant to blight.

More recently, the American elm (*Ulmus americana*) has been driven to virtual extinction by an introduced fungal pathogen, known as Dutch elm disease (*Ophiostoma ulmi*).[6]

White pine blister rust, a fungus from northern Europe, is killing off the white bark pine trees in almost every high-elevation national park in the American West. This is not simply an aesthetic matter, as these trees grow where other conifers do not, holding the soil, regulating snow melt, and producing nuts that feed numerous birds and mammals. They appear to be essential to the survival of grizzly bears in such areas. Thirty years of effort and nearly 2 million liters of herbicide have failed to control white pine blister rust in Yellowstone National Park.

The health impacts of invasive species are substantial. According to one estimate, the cost of introduced disease to human, livestock, and crop plant health is more than $41 billion per year in the United States.[7]

THE ECONOMIC COSTS

In the mid-nineteenth century, wine was the second-largest export from France, after textiles. Its production accounted for the employment of a third of the French population and about one-sixth of government revenues. But the French wine industry was nearly eliminated by an invasive alien species from North America. During this period, a few tiny aphids were brought to France on vines from the United States and spread quickly throughout most of France.[8]

Ultimately, the solution came from grafting the traditional European vines onto American vine roots that were resistant to the aphid. This illustrates the critical difference between a non-native species and an invasive non-native species. The American grapevine that was imported remains a domestic species that poses no threat to wild ecosystems or other domestic species, whereas the aphid was invasive and destructive, spreading at will and under no form of human control.

The probability that any one introduced species will become invasive may be low, but the costs of the damage that results, and of control of the species that do become invasive, can be extremely high (as was the case during the recent invasion of eastern Canada by the brown spruce longhorn beetle, which threatens the Canadian timber industry).

The Asian long-horned beetle is one of the newest and most serious invasive species threats in the United States. Originating in northeastern Asia, it arrived in America in packing crates made of low-quality timber (i.e., timber too infested with pests for other uses). The beetles found a congenial home among maples, elders, elms, chestnuts, and other trees. Outbreaks were reported in and around Chicago as early as 1992, and there is evidence that they became established in New York as the result of an infestation reported in Brooklyn in August 1996. Formally known as *Anoplophora glabripennis,* the species was subsequently found in many other parts of New York. One scientist predicted that if the Asian long-horned beetle became established, it could wipe out a quarter of the shade trees growing in U.S. cities. It is no coincidence that cities are its main target, because urban trees often are stressed by pollution, compact the ground growing around them, lack traditional nutrients from leaf litter, suffer shortages of water because of the concrete often found around their root systems, and miss out on the benefits provided by predatory species such as woodpeckers, cuckoos, and wasps.

In New York, nearly four thousand trees had to be replaced by less susceptible species at a cost of $10 million. The Asian longhorn beetle has already destroyed more than seven thousand hardwood trees in New York and Chicago, and as it continues to spread, it could affect up to $600 billion worth of urban trees over the next thirty years.

Other outbreaks were reported in California in 1997, leading to an interim ban on the importation of Chinese goods packed in untreated timber crates. This action was justified on the basis that the number of insects found in materials imported from China increased from 1 percent of all interceptions in 1987 to 20 percent in 1996. Today, all solid-wood packing material from China must be certified as free of bark (under which insects may lurk) and heat-treated, fumigated, or treated with preservatives. Of course, the materials found were just the tip of the iceberg, with some 1,300 overworked quarantine officers responsible for inspecting 410,000 planes and over 50,000 ships. Although they intercepted alien species on nearly 50,000 occasions, it is highly likely that at least tens of thousands more entered the country uninspected. The U.S. Department of Agriculture has established an Animal and Plant Health Inspection Service (APHIS) to inspect the 14 million shipping containers that arrive annually at U.S. ports. It is able to inspect only 2 percent of them, yet finds dangerous exotic insects on or in wooden packing material more than 400 times a year.

In Louisiana, Formosan termites (*Coptotermes formosanus*) have been eating the expansion joints between many sections of the floodwall along the Mississippi River, tunneling through a thick plastic barrier to get to them. This damage amounts to $300 million a year in New Orleans.

Zebra mussels cost U.S. industry about $100 million per year, primarily by clogging pipes and reducing water flow to lakeside power plants. The zebra mussel, through its filtration and over-growth activities, is predicted to cause the extinction of about ninety species of freshwater mussels in the Mississippi Basin within the next fifty years. According to one study, it is worth spending up to $324,000 a year to stop zebra mussels from contaminating a lake adjoining a large power plant.[9]

The yellow star thistle (*Centaurea solstialis*) is an invasive species in California that is unpalatable to cattle, leading to an annual loss of $7.65 million in lost livestock forage and an additional $9.45 million in expenditures made by ranchers to control the species. Even worse, it depletes soil moisture, with an estimated cost of somewhere between $16 million and $75 million a year in the Sacramento watershed alone.[10]

The golden apple snail (*Pomacea canaliculata*) was intentionally introduced into Southeast Asia to serve as a potential food source, but instead it had numerous negative impacts; among these was its tendency to feed on young rice seedlings, which cost rice farmers in the Philippines at least US$425 million per year.

Added to the direct economic costs of management of invasives are the costs associated with their indirect environmental consequences and other nonmarket values. For example, invasives may cause changes in ecological services by disturbing the operation of the hydrological cycle, including flood control and water supply, waste assimilation, recycling of nutrients, conservation and regeneration of soils, pollination of crops, and seed dispersal. Such services have both current use value and option value (the potential value of such services in the future). For example, in the South African fynbos, a form of vegetation unique to that part of the world, the establishment of invasive tree species has decreased water supplies for nearby communities and increased fire hazards. Invasive alien woody plants in South Africa consume an estimated 3,300 million cubic meters of water per year more than the native species. Some catchments lose over 90 percent of their water to the invasive species.[11] This has justified government expenditures of US$40 million per year for manual and chemical control.

An alternative estimate puts the annual cost of invasive weed species in the United States at $23.4 billion—a figure that incorporates other values, such as yield reduction in crops. The researchers who quoted this estimate claim that "[i]f we had been able to assign monetary values to species extinctions and losses in biodiversity, ecosystems services, and aesthetics, the costs of destructive non-indigenous species would undoubtedly be several times higher than $137 billion per year."[12]

THE DAMAGE TO NATIVE SPECIES
AND ECOSYSTEMS

All parts of the world suffer from invasive species, but isolated continents and islands with a long history of independent evolution are particularly vulnerable. Perhaps the most dramatic example is Australia, where an estimated 27,000 non-native species have been introduced since human settlement, of which about 10 percent have become established in the wild. These invasive alien species are threatening more than fifty native species with extinction.

Cane toads are among Australia's most troublesome invasive alien species (as viewers of the film that sparked the creation of this book can attest). The annual rate of progress on the toad-invasion front has increased about five-fold since the toads first arrived. First introduced to Queensland in 1935 in hopes of controlling insect pests in sugar cane fields, the cane toad now occupies over 1 million square kilometers of tropical and subtropical Australia. The cane toad is expanding its range across tropical Australia and has invaded Kakadu National Park, a World Heritage site where it is having a severely detrimental impact on the northern quoll (*Dasyurus hallucatus*). It is a native marsupial predator, which would likely attack cane toads at any time they were found. Yet the cane toad is highly poisonous: Quolls have been found dead with reddened gums, a certain indication of cane toad poisoning.[13] Other evidence indicates that the cane toads also lead to the decline of native frogs.

Australia has an estimated 4–12 million feral cats, on a continent that previously had only marsupial predators. In the Kimberley Mountains in northwestern Australia, these cats are eating an estimated 300 million small mammals per year, hitting small nocturnal marsupials especially hard. In thinly populated northern Australia, thought to be rich in biodiversity, field biologists are finding small native mammals exceedingly rare. One recent study took an average of a thousand trap-nights to capture three mammals. But in places where dingos reside (dingos are wild dogs derived from domesticated or semi-domesticated species brought in by aborigines), the numbers of cats are much lower—a situation that is expected to result in larger numbers of small marsupials and reptiles. Nature has shown a remarkable capacity to adapt from disruptions, but only if the native species are allowed to survive.

The accidental introduction of ragwort (*Senecio jacobaea*) had disastrous consequences in late-nineteenth century New Zealand. Like many such species, it quickly became a pest, owing to noxious alkaloids that make it dangerous for grazing animals to eat. Even honey made from its flowers is poisonous. New Zealand farmers therefore looked to poisons to control the species, and the government recommended sodium chlorate as an effective weed killer. One tiny problem: When the chemical mixes with organic material such as the fibers of a farmer's working clothes, it becomes extremely dangerous and will detonate at the first sign of a spark or glowing cigarette, or even simply a shock or knock. As a result, many New Zealand farmers found their pants catching on fire, leading to numerous injuries and even a few deaths.[14] Today, biological controls—mostly insects imported from the European original habitat of ragwort—are proving much more successful. No longer do New Zealand's farmers need to worry about exploding trousers.

But these isolated islands can also be the source of invasives. The New Zealand flatworm (*Arthurdendyus tringulatus*) is a voracious earthworm predator that was accidentally introduced to Edinburgh in 1965 and spread across the U.K. and has now become a major force in reducing earthworm abundance in many gardens throughout the region. It lives exclusively on earthworms and destroys the ecosystem services that earthworms provide, including aeration of soil and provision of prey to native bird and mammal species. (Europe has also exported worms.)

Kudzu (*Pueraria montana*) was intentionally introduced into the United States from Japan as an ornamental plant in 1876. It has now become a significant pest in much of the country, from Nebraska to Texas across to Florida and up to Maine. In addition to choking out native vegetation, it is about twice as efficient as other plants in fixing atmospheric nitrogen. It is one of the leading plant sources of isoprene, a hydrocarbon that reacts with oxides of nitrogen to form ozone in the presence of sunlight. By producing excess nitrogen, kudzu is not only providing fertilizer to other fast-growing invasive plants but also adding runoff nitrogen to streams and rivers, causing algal blooms that deplete oxygen and lead to hypoxic zones deadly to fish. The plant now covers some 3 million hectares in the United States.[15]

Isolated lakes are also highly vulnerable to invasion. One dramatic example is the invasion of Lake Victoria by the Nile perch, leading to the loss of some 70 percent of the cichlid species of fish in the lake—perhaps the worst extinction episode in this century.

Another example of a purposeful introduction gone wrong is the extensive stocking program that introduced African tilapia (*Oreochromis*) into Lake Nicaragua in the 1980s, resulting in the decline of native populations of fish and leading to the imminent collapse of one of the world's most distinctive freshwater ecosystems. The African tilapia found Lake Nicaragua a very congenial habitat, one where they could grow rapidly, feed on a wide range of plants, fish, and other organisms, and form large schools that can migrate long distances. Further, they are maternal mouth brooders, so a single female can colonize a new environment by carrying her young in her mouth. They are also larger than the native fish and replace them in territorial conflicts. Even worse, these invaders have proven adaptable to salt-water habitats and may invade Nicaragua's coastal zone as well, affecting productive marine fisheries and valuable estuarine nursery grounds. As one study has pointed out, the alteration of Lake Nicaragua's ecosystem is likely to have effects on the planktonic community and primary productivity of the entire lake, destroying native fish populations and perhaps leading to unanticipated consequences.[16]

No continents are immune to invasives. European cheat grass (*Bromus tectorum*) is dramatically changing the vegetation and fauna of many natural ecosystems, invading and spreading throughout the shrub-steppe habitat of the Great Basin in Idaho and Utah and predisposing the invaded habitat to fires. Before the cheat grass invaded, fires burned only once every 60 to 110 years, enabling shrubs to become well established. But fires coming every three to five years have led to a significant decline in shrubs and other vegetation, establishing cheat grass monocultures on 5 million hectares in this region. Animals dependent on shrubs and other original vegetation have been reduced or eliminated, demonstrating the cascading effects of invasive species.[17]

The shrub *Impatiens glandulifera* was introduced to the U.K. in 1839 and has now spread across much of the region, especially along riverbanks and damp woodlands. It has also invaded New Zealand, Canada, and the United States. Where it spreads, it can reduce native-plant diversity by up to 25 percent. When it dies down each winter, its bulky stalks can clog streams, causing flooding and leaving river banks bare and prone to erosion.

Another study provides several examples of the scale of current invasives:

> North American seed and nursery catalogues offer over 59,000 plant species and varieties for sale to national and international markets; the rate of invasions in San Francisco Bay has accelerated from an average of one new species established every 55 weeks

during the period 1851–1960 to one new species every 14 weeks during the period 1961–1995; and microbial pathogens, mostly viruses and virus-like organisms, accompanied more than half of the apple and potato accessions inspected in quarantine in the United States between 1985 and 1994.[18]

DISRUPTION OF AQUATIC ECOSYSTEMS

In the freshwater ecosystems of the Netherlands, the native shrimp *Gammarus duebeni* is being wiped out by a voracious shrimp species (*Dikerogammarus villosus*) that is invading from Eastern Europe and the Ukraine through the Danube-Main canal, which opened in 1992. The alien simply eats the native shrimp, as well as another invasive species, *G. tigrinus*, a fast-breeding species from North America that probably reached Europe in ship ballast water. Thus an invasive species of shrimp is consuming both a native species and another invasive species.

Most of the high-elevation lakes in the American West have become renowned as a paradise for trout fishing. But trout are an alien species in these habitats, having been introduced by the millions from hatcheries by the California Department of Fish and Game. The ecological impact of this introduction has been profound, leading to catastrophic declines in some species of amphibians. Trout are voracious predators of species such as the mountain yellow-legged frog, feeding on both tadpoles and adults. This species is especially vulnerable to such predation because it spends virtually its entire life in water. The species is now being proposed for listing as endangered. Enabling the frog to recover to a healthy population level will require eliminating all trout from many of the Sierra lakes. It is expected that the removal of trout from these lakes will cause vociferous protest from some fishermen and local communities.

In Yosemite National Park in California, non-native species of trout have been widely introduced. The mountain yellow-legged frog (*Rana muscosa*), Pacific tree frog (*Hila regilla*), mountain garter snake (*Thamnophis elegans*), and Sierra garter snake (*Thamnophis couchi*) were all strongly negatively correlated with the presence of the introduced trout, indicating that these invasive species have had a profound impact on the reptiles and amphibians and, through them, the ecosystems in these regions. In the western United States, more than 60 percent of all naturally fishless lakes, many located within national parks and wilderness areas, now contain non-native trout, leading to elimination of amphibian and reptile populations, changes in zooplankton and benthic macro-invertebrate species composition and size structure, and alteration of ecosystem processes such as nutrient cycling.[19]

The northern pike (*Esox lucius*) has invaded rivers in Alaska and is devastating native species of salmon. While the northern pike occurs naturally in some parts of Alaska, it was introduced to the salmon rich south-central area in the 1950s, probably by a fisherman who brought it to Bulchitna Lake. Flooding in the 1980s subsequently spread the pike into the streams of the Susitna and Matanuska river basins. Pike have now occupied at least a dozen lakes and four rivers in some of the richest salmon and trout habitat in the American Northwest.

In the United States, which has the most comprehensive data on freshwater species, 37 percent of freshwater fish, 67 percent of mussels, 51 percent of crayfish, and 40 percent of amphibians are threatened or have become extinct. At least 138 fish species have been introduced into the United States, and 54 native fish species are threatened or endangered by them.[20] Studies of the introduction of non-native fish in Europe, North America, Australia, and New Zealand reveal that 77 percent of them resulted in the drastic reduction or elimination of native fish species. In North America alone, 27 species and 13 subspecies of native fish became extinct in the last century largely due to the introduction of non-native fish.

Dramatic Changes to Island Ecosystems

Much of the world's biodiversity is found on islands. But ecosystems that are geographically or evolutionarily isolated—notably oceanic islands—are known to be particularly vulnerable to invasion. Such systems have been isolated over millions of years, thus favoring the evolution of endemic species (those found nowhere else). However, the evolutionary processes associated with isolation make such species especially vulnerable to competitors, predators, pathogens, and parasites from other areas. Multi-island states like Indonesia and groups of islands like the Galápagos can be extremely vulnerable to transfers from one island to another because the islands, even those relatively close to one another, may each have different endemics.

Plants also cause problems on islands. As just one example, the tree *Miconia calvescens* replaced more than 70 percent of the forest canopy of Tahiti over a fifty-year time span, starting with a few trees in two botanical gardens. Some 40 to 50 of the 107 plant species endemic to the island of Tahiti are believed to be on the verge of extinction primarily due to this invasion.[21]

The arrival of humans on oceanic islands has precipitated a wave of extinctions among the native birds on the islands, with the magnitude of the extinction process varying markedly among avifaunas. One study shows that the probability that a bird species has disappeared from each of 220 oceanic islands is positively correlated with the number of non-native predatory mammal species established on those islands after European colonization, and that the effect of these predators is greater on the species found only on those islands.[22] Even greater extinctions took place before European colonization; at least two thousand species of Pacific Island birds are known to have become extinct after Polynesian people arrived, along with rats and pigs.

The brown tree snake was probably introduced into Guam during World War II, as a stowaway on a military cargo ship. It subsequently led to the local extirpation or extinction of nine of the eleven endemic species of birds and four of the twelve endemic lizards. It also had an economic impact, causing some 1,600 electrical power outages between 1978 and 1997, which cost the economy about US$4.5 million per year.

Another study has shown that the introduction of Arctic foxes (*Alopex lagopus*) to the Aleutian archipelago induced strong shifts in plant productivity and community structure via a previously unknown pathway. By preying on sea birds, foxes reduced nutrient transport from ocean to land, affecting soil fertility and transforming grasslands to dwarf shrub/forb–dominated ecosystems.[23] This indicates the potential impact of invasive alien species that prey on seabirds, which includes the introduction of rats on many Pacific islands.

Goats introduced on San Clemente Island, California, have exterminated eight endemic species of plants and endangered eight others.[24]

In Hawaii during the 1950s, three predatory land snails were enlisted to combat the giant African snail, an invasive species that has been a notorious agricultural pest throughout Southeast Asia and the Pacific. But one of the introduced snails, *Euglandina rosea*, also feeds on native snails, several of which are now extinct. Thus species introduced for justifiable economic and ecological reasons—to control a harmful alien invasive species—can themselves become problems and even lead to the extinction of native species.

After many years of general silence on the topic of invasive alien species, the World Wildlife Fund (WWF) has come out strongly in support of the eradication of rabbits from Macquarie Island, near Antarctica, because their grazing of grasses is causing landslides and destroying nesting sites for penguins and albatrosses. Introduced to the island by European sealers in the 1800s, the population has now reached more than 100,000, threatening the breeding habitat of 850,000 pairs of royal penguins as well as almost 4 million seabirds, including two threatened albatross species. Invasive rats and mice add to the problem, eating young seabirds in their nests. Macquarie is on the World Heritage List.

THE DAMAGE TO ONE COUNTRY—CHINA

The chief economist at the Chinese Ministry of Agriculture, Zhu Xiuyan, has underlined the links between global trade, economic integration, and invasive alien species. He has concluded that eleven major invasive species in China bring economic losses amounting to US$7 billion per year, while the Chinese ecologist Li Wenhua has concluded that the total annual loss has reached about US$15 billion, 1.36 percent of the GDP. Canada goldenrod (*Solidago canadensis*) was imported in 1935 to Shanghai and Nanjin as a courtyard flower but has now spread throughout the country, replacing native species; at least thirty local species in Shanghai have disappeared because of the Canada goldenrod. Crayfish introduced from Mexico have spread widely throughout China, affecting the survival of native fish and shrimp as well as undermining dams and rice field bunds. The Mediterranean fruit fly (*Ceratitis capitita*) has become a significant crop pest in southern China.

A major problem is that China has no effective legislation preventing and controlling invasive alien species, though of course it is subject to relevant international conventions such as the

Convention on Biological Diversity and the World Trade Agreement on sanitary and phytosanitary measures. New legislation is being enacted in several provinces so as to restrict the importation and sale of non-native species that are likely to become invasive. China is also increasing its investments in biological controls, using native species against the non-natives.

In China, fish constitute a particularly important invasives problem. In the 1970s, more than 30 alien species of fish were found in Dianchi Lake, reducing the number of native species from 25 to just 8 over a period of twenty years.[25]

One Chinese study identified 283 invasive alien species, including 19 micro-organisms, 18 aquatic plants, 170 terrestrial plants, 25 aquatic invertebrates, 33 terrestrial invertebrates, 3 amphibians and reptiles, 10 fish, and 5 mammals. Of these, 55 percent originated from the Western Hemisphere, 22 percent from Europe, 10 percent from Asia, and 8 percent from Africa. About half of the invasive alien plants were intentionally introduced, as were 25 percent of invasive animal species.[26] Perhaps worse, new efforts are being made to introduce alien species with insufficient attention to the management of the potential hazards of such species. All micro-organisms were unintentionally introduced, through timber, seedlings, flower pots, or soils; 75.3 percent of invasive animals arrived through commodity or transportation facilities that were inadequately protected by quarantine systems. The authors of this study call for more effective quarantine measures and more effective systems of risk assessment. It is highly likely that China has far more invasive species than has been documented to date.

The salt marsh grass known as *Spartina alterniflora* is a native of eastern North America that was introduced to China in 1979 as a means of controlling soil erosion. It has now spread across southeastern China, choking estuaries, crowding out native grasses, and reducing feed and habitat for fish and migratory birds.[27]

THE BIG PICTURE

Philosophical issues cannot be separated from technical ones in the field of invasive alien species. Human dimensions must be considered at every stage in the discussion. One critical issue is the definition of "native," involving at least three perspectives: time scales, boundaries, and the role of human agency.

Regarding time scales, species are constantly expanding and contracting, sometimes with human help. Species recovery programs often seek to reintroduce native species that subsequently were lost (e.g., the Arabian oryx, the wolf in certain parts of the United States, and the beaver in Scotland). Are programs like these ecologically valid, or do they represent a human-assisted form of "invasion"? The answer may depend on the time scale we choose to consider.

In a similar way, boundaries are an issue where countries are contiguous with others, enabling species to move back and forth with or without human help. Because scientific understanding of species distributions is still very spotty, new discoveries of species in an area where they were unknown before may simply reflect insufficient prior knowledge. The concept of "native" commits us to support ecosystems reflecting a particular environmental and climatic state that is dynamic, highlighting the irony that today's growing concern about non-native species comes at a time when climates are changing rapidly. Furthermore, speciation and development of biotic communities depend on organisms invading novel habitats and, in some instances, hybridizing.[28]

Taking all these considerations into account, some scientists argue that the very concepts of "native" and "alien" are based on value judgements associated with a selective time frame, and an arbitrary view of which types of humans can legitimately act as modes of dispersal.[29]

Thus conservation and preservation clearly are value-driven activities, leading to paradoxical situations where considerable "artificial" inputs of management effort are devoted to maintaining "natural" habitats. At a time when human influences are increasingly fragmenting habitats, this effort will inevitably change the components and organization of ecological communities; thus the issue of the specialized roles of individual species may have diverted attention from the more interesting study of ecological flexibility and adaptation to changing conditions.

Does this mean that concern about invasive species and their disruptive impact on environments is misplaced or groundless? Not at all. Indeed, thoughtful study of the big picture of world ecology provides an essential context within which to understand the dynamics of evolution and the role played in the process by all living species—including humans.

Dangerous Strangers

How Rogue Species Threaten Our Endangered Species

Leda Huta and Greg Kuether

Leda Huta has served as the executive director of the Endangered Species Coalition since 2006. The Endangered Species Coalition is a nonprofit organization that includes more than four hundred conservation, scientific, faith, recreation, and business groups in forty-seven states. Huta has sixteen years of environmental and consumer nonprofit experience, having successfully managed and fundraised for grassroots, national, and international projects. Her work has encompassed a range of issues including species protection, forest conservation, energy, environment and health, and green businesses.

Most recently, Huta was the acting executive director for Finding Species, a nonprofit that uses photography as a tool to protect species biodiversity from the United States to the Amazon. Previous to that, she worked for the Resource Conservation Alliance to protect forests by advancing alternatives to the commercial use of ancient-forest wood products.

Huta has served on numerous boards for environmental and community organizations, and she is one of the co-founders of EcoWomen, a community of women working or interested in the environmental field who foster networking and collaboration for a healthy environment. She speaks Ukrainian and Spanish and has a Bachelor of Science degree from the University of Toronto with a double major in environmental science and environment and resource management and a minor in zoology.

Greg Kuether started working with the Endangered Species Coalition in August 2009 as the volunteer executive assistant. Before coming to the ESC, he worked in multimedia development. Three years ago he decided to take his love for the environment beyond the personal level. He enrolled in the Johns Hopkins University and received a Master of Science degree in environmental sciences and policy in May 2009. Greg lives in Baltimore, Maryland, with his partner Kevin, his rescue greyhound Speed, and two "terror-kitties," Loki and Gebo, in their solar-powered row home. He continues to experiment with finding vegetables that grow well in containers.

In "Dangerous Strangers," Leda and Greg focus on one important aspect of the invasive species problem—the danger that invaders pose to native species that may already be on the brink of extinction. As they explain, unless we get the challenge of rogue species under control, some of our world's most treasured denizens may vanish forever.

In 1973, Americans decided that we wanted our lands to teem with the incredibly diverse wildlife that our country once had. And we determined we would take some pretty extraordinary steps to make that happen. We passed the Endangered Species Act—a landmark law to bring back the wildlife, plants, birds, and fish that were holding on to existence by the very *slimmest* of margins. And, to bring back these species, we realized we would need to bring back their old stomping grounds as well. For to truly recover species to a semblance of their once glorious populations, they'd need their habitat.

It is a difficult process, this saving of more than 1,300 species. Some have been pushed so far to the edge that their species' hopes rest on the amorous pairings of just a handful of couples. And the recovery of a species is slowed by any number of threats. One such threat has become acutely insidious and difficult to thwart in the past few decades—invasive species.

Endangered island wildlife is particularly imperiled. It is not a coincidence that Hawaii, overrun with invasive species, has the country's largest number of endangered species. Some of the nation's most recent extinctions have happened here. Invasive mosquitoes carrying avian malaria and avian pox are killing off Hawaii's native land birds. Similarly, the introduced brown tree snake has driven almost all of Guam's native birds to extinction.

While islands offer the most extreme case studies of what can happen when an invasive species is introduced, the severe threat from invasives spans the nation and the globe. According to the U.S. Fish and Wildlife Service, invasive species threaten more than 40 percent of U.S. endangered species.[1] Globally, invasive species are among the top five threats for endangered mammals, birds, reptiles, and amphibians.[2]

Whether introduced purposefully or unknowingly, invasive species wreak havoc on the most vulnerable wildlife. Invasive species have one shared trait: Like houseguests who overstay their welcome, they have made themselves too comfortable in a new home where they most certainly do not belong. And they're making life difficult for the home's inhabitants.

Apart from that commonality, invasive species' methods for undoing an endangered species vary greatly. Some invasive species prefer the direct approach when harming imperiled wildlife and plants. Others harm not the endangered species itself but, rather, its surroundings—altering its landscape, destroying its food source, outcompeting it for water, or eliminating its shelter.

THE DIRECT ASSAULT
The Burmese Python: Why Florida Shouldn't Be Everyone's Second Home

When does a mere pet become a threat? When it is the Burmese python. Of all the invasive species that favor the direct approach, the Burmese python stirs perhaps the greatest passions from humans.

Likely introduced into the Florida Everglades from the pet trade, the Burmese python has quickly made itself at home in its new environment. The first confirmation of Burmese pythons breeding in the Everglades was in 2003.[3] Estimates for the number of pythons now calling the Everglades home vary, with some scientists believing it to be more than 30,000.[4] And, unfortunately, there are several reasons why this population may increase.

Pet owners are likely still releasing them. The number of Burmese pythons imported into the United States for the pet trade has skyrocketed to about 10,000 per year.[5] Supplementing these imported pythons is the domestic trade—estimated to be much higher. Even if pet owners stop intentionally releasing the snakes, unintentional releases may persist. In fact, reptile-breeding centers near the Everglades that were destroyed by Hurricane Andrew may have been the original source of released pet pythons.[6]

Once it arrives in the Everglades, the python, a native of southern and southwestern Asia, does quite well. It can live twenty-five to forty years. The largest recorded python in the Everglades measured sixteen feet and weighed 152 pounds. A long, healthy life can produce a lot of babies. The largest found clutch of python eggs in the Everglades comprised a whopping 107.[7]

And while Burmese pythons are now found only in Florida, global climate change could be a game changer for this species. If current climate projections hold true, the pythons could spread across one-third of the United States. Given their long life and high birth rate, a continued source of new pythons from the pet trade together with an expanding range due to global warming could easily spell disaster for the endangered species in the pythons' wake.

Their only threats in the Florida Everglades come from the Florida panther and American alligator. However, this is a double-edged sword because pythons also prey on these two species. The

American alligator is a successfully recovered endangered species, while the Florida panther is one of the most endangered species in North America. In addition to having a taste for these two endangered species, the python is impacting other imperiled wildlife. One study estimates that a total of seventy-one federally or state listed endangered or threatened species are at an increased risk of extinction if the python continues its spread.[8] These range from diminutive Floridian species that are among the most endangered in the country, such as the Key Largo cotton mouse, the Key Largo woodrat, and the Lower Keys marsh rabbit to larger species, such as the Key deer, Florida black bear and American crocodile, all of whom may fall prey to the python.

Red Fire Ants:
The Gruesome Travelers

Not all invasive species that directly attack endangered wildlife are big and burly. Some, such as the red fire ant, have tremendous power in their sheer numbers. Posing an unpleasant nuisance to humans, it can be deadly to endangered and threatened species.

Red fire ants are thought to have arrived in the United States around 1940 in Alabama, via ships.[9] There were already native fire ant colonies in the southeastern United States, so not much attention was given to this new arrival. By the 1950s, however, these introduced red fire ants from South America became the dominant species and were spreading roughly a hundred miles a year.[10]

These little insects do know how to travel. If a fire ant hill becomes flooded, the ants form a raft out of their bodies and float to a new location. More typically, they are transported in shipments of hay, soil, or sod. This has resulted in fire ant introduction into such places as California. The ants will also spread after queen ants mate and fly away, creating nests where they land.[11]

Red fire ants are aggressive and deadly. They kill their prey by swarming and stinging it. The weakened prey is eventually eaten. When fire ants come to town, the biodiversity there can plummet. In one case, fire ants were implicated in a *92 percent* decrease in waterbirds.[12] Initially, scientists believed that red fire ants targeted only ground nesting birds, but one study has shown that they also pose a threat to songbirds.[13] Red fire ants are killing a number of endangered bird chicks, including the Mississippi sandhill crane, a highly endangered bird with only about twenty-five nesting pairs remaining in the wild; the golden-cheeked warbler, found nesting in Texas in small groups; and the black-capped vireo, a songbird from the south-central United States.[14]

Red fire ants also pose a threat to a species most of us would not imagine could be killed by an insect. Fire ants can kill imperiled loggerhead and green sea turtle hatchlings.[15] Allowed to reach adulthood, these sea turtle hatchlings would have incredible lives ahead of them—split between land and the ocean and pursuing a migration route that for loggerheads can span more than 7,500 miles. But, when red fire ants have their way, these hatchlings' nomadic lives are cut short. The ants burrow into the turtle nests and once the eggs begin to hatch, the ants attack the hatchlings. On Sanibel Island off the Florida coast, fire ants may in fact be the greatest threat to nesting sea turtles.

The Zebra Mussel:
Suffocating Its Way Through American Waterways

Invasive species that attack imperiled wildlife aren't limited to land; they can be found in water also. The Great Lakes have become a veritable invasive species soup. Invasives such as the bloody red shrimp, spiny waterflea, fishhook waterflea, fourspine stickleback, round goby, sea lamprey, Eurasian ruffe, humpbacked pea-clam, quagga mussel, and, of course, the zebra mussel have found their way into the Great Lakes from far-flung locations around the world.

The tiny zebra mussel is thought to have entered the United States in 1988 at Lake St. Clair, in Michigan. Native to Eastern Europe and Asia, it arrived in the ballast waters of ships. Since then, zebra mussels have spread to all of the Great Lakes and their tributaries as well as to 230 other lakes throughout the Midwest.[16]

Stopping them won't be easy. Zebra mussels have no known predators in U.S. waters. A single mussel is capable of producing *1 million eggs*. And larval mussels are impossible to see with the naked eye, so they are often spread via ship ballast, bait buckets, and even scuba equipment from infested waterways. The situation could accurately be described as an all-out invasion.

This zebra mussel invasion is threatening the survival of native U.S. freshwater mussels and clams. Zebra mussels like to attach to hard substrates. So they have been attaching themselves to our native species. There is a report of up to ten thousand zebra mussels having been found attached to a single native mollusk. This kind of attachment is too close for comfort for the poor native mollusks. Unable to move due to the crush of attached mollusks, they are essentially smothered to death.

All American native clams are gone from Lake St. Clair and from a portion of Lake Erie. Of the 281 native species of freshwater mollusks, 19 are extinct, 21 are thought extinct, 77 are endangered, 43 are threatened, and 72 are of special concern. These include the American unionid clam and the Higgins eye mussel.[17] The zebra mussel is not the sole factor contributing to the extinction of clam species, but one study indicates that the invasive mussel increases the extinction rate by a factor of ten.[18]

In addition to the zebra mussel, a new invasive species is devouring its way up the Mississippi. The voracious Asian carp has thus far not entered the Great Lakes, and the federal government plans to keep it that way. In February 2010, the government presented a five-year blueprint for the Great Lakes area, a $2.2 billion plan to take a "zero tolerance policy" toward future invasive species entering the region.[19]

LOVE NOT WAR

The barred tiger salamander directly harms an endangered species, but in an entirely unique way. Its native habitat ranges from central Nebraska to northeastern Mexico, but it was introduced into California approximately sixty years ago as fishing bait and released into the same vernal pools occupied by the endemic California tiger salamander. The latter is a highly endangered species in the United States with only six known populations. Soon the barred tiger salamander began mating with the California tiger salamander, creating a hybrid salamander.[20]

Now, the native and endangered California tiger salamander faces competition from the invasive barred tiger salamander *and* from the hybrid. Usually, a hybrid is not a concern, because it tends to be a weaker version of its precursors that is not capable of reproduction. The hybrid of the barred and California tiger salamanders is an exception to the rule.[21]

These hybrids not only can reproduce but are larger, have a bigger jaw, and exhibit a more aggressive nature. As a result, they fiercely compete with the native California tiger salamander for food *and* cannibalize it.[22] These hearty eaters have also been implicated as a threat to the endangered Santa Cruz long-toed salamander, found in only two counties in California, as well as to the endangered California red-legged frog, highlighted in a famous short story by Mark Twain.[23]

Despite the hybrids' threat to three endangered species, the issue of their own protection has been raised. Since the hybrid salamanders share 50 percent of the native salamander's genetic makeup, should they, too, be classified as an endangered species?[24] Some scientists believe this is one strategy for preserving the California tiger salamander. Of course, we can probably guess what the Santa Cruz long-toed salamander and the California red-legged frog might say.

Going After Hearth and Home

Perhaps a more widespread threat to endangered species and the biodiversity of the nation comes from those invasive species that alter habitats. Although they don't directly kill imperiled wildlife, their assault on habitats eliminates needed food, shelter, water, and other requirements for survival.

Balsam Woolly Adelgids: Ladies of Destruction

Some invasive mini-assassins may be less gruesome than the red fire ants, but their impacts are no less sad. Endangered species in the Appalachian fir forests are facing a threat from an invader less than 1 millimeter in size. The balsam woolly adelgid is an aphid-like insect that is decimating old-growth fir stands in the Appalachian Mountains.[25]

First discovered in North Carolina in 1957, the balsam woolly adelgid probably arrived on nursery stock that was first imported into Canada from Europe. The insects progressed their way across stands of fir trees. By today's estimates, they have destroyed 95 percent of the southern Appalachian region's Frasier firs—a beloved and coveted Christmas tree in the United States.[26]

The adelgid launches massive attacks with populations of 100 to 200 individuals per square inch. They spread easily in part because, in the United States, all of the insects are females—they essentially clone themselves. And they can be carried long distances by the wind, nearly thirty miles at a time.

Once an adelgid arrives at a tree, its attack causes the tree to develop a condition called "gouting," similar to arthritis in humans. Swellings on the terminal growth twigs occur, and in many instances the tops of the trees begin to curl downward (much like curling in of fingers in extreme cases of arthritis). Trees affected by this condition face a slow death than can take tortuous years.[27]

Once destroyed by the adelgid, the dead fir tree causes an opening in the forest canopy. And when the canopy opens up, the moist mossy forest-floor covering dries up—altering the landscape of this habitat. Not only is the Frasier fir itself a species of special concern, but the forest habitat that it comprises is home to many species that are rare, endemic, endangered, and/or of special concern. Among the forest habitat's rare and endemic species (found only in this region), two are endangered—the spruce fir moss spider and the Carolina flying squirrel.

The spruce fir moss spider, a tiny tarantula measuring 0.1 to 0.15 inches, lives only in the humid moss mats of the high forests of the Appalachians. The extremely rare Carolina flying squirrel, meanwhile, plays a key role in the Appalachian ecosystem by spreading around truffles that help trees absorb water and other nutrients.[28] Losing their forest habitat home would be a death knell to both of these unique species.

White Pine Blister Rot: A Grizzly Encounter

The mighty grizzly bear may be thought of as a majestic hunter catching salmon in the middle of rushing rapids. However, in the

Lower 48, the grizzly depends on a much smaller food source—the humble pine nut from the whitebark pine tree. Unfortunately, this tree is threatened by the white pine blister rot—a fungus that attacks its bark, causing blisters and cankers to form and eventually killing the tree.

Taking a somewhat circuitous route to arrive in the United States, likely traveling on nursery stock from Germany to France to British Columbia, white pine blister rot was first noticed in the Greater Yellowstone Area in the 1940s. Since then, infection rates have soared. And once a whitebark pine grove is affected, there is usually a 99 percent infection rate and a 100 percent mortality rate.[29] Climate change may make things worse, helping the white pine blister rot to spread further.

The loss of the tree means the loss of the whitebark pine nut— a food that is extremely important to the grizzly bear. Pine nuts are large and have a high fat content. This fat provides the energy needed for survival during hibernation.[30] In some regions of the Greater Yellowstone Area, the pine nuts make up the whole diet of the bears. But once the white pine blister rot infects a tree, it decreases seed production and size. Death rates among grizzly bears increase as pine nut availability decreases.[31]

The Buffelgrass: A Blaze of Devastation

Insects and fungi aren't the only enemies to key endangered-species habitats. Plants can be equally destructive. Buffelgrass—an invasive grass that has spread across the southwestern United States— is one such example. Its native region stretches from Africa across to India, but it was purposely brought into the United States to be used as grazing material for cattle ranchers in the 1930s and tested for soil erosion control from then through the 1980s. The public began to take notice of buffelgrass in the early 1990s after it ran rampant throughout the Sonoran Desert—specifically, as a result of warm-season rainfall that was above average.[32]

Buffelgrass, which is highly flammable, has brought about a frightening change to the Sonoran Desert: It drastically increases the frequency of fires in this area. The fires destroy native vegetation—and because buffelgrass is extremely hardy, it is the primary species that repopulates the desert after a fire.[33]

By significantly altering the habitat, buffelgrass harms endangered and threatened species unique to the Sonoran region. The cactus ferruginous pygmy owl nests in the region's famous saguaro cactus—frequently depicted in American cowboy movies. But the fires are weakening and killing these cacti homes. They are also reducing the availability of the owl's prey.[34]

The desert tortoise is also in trouble. This unique species spends 95 percent of its life underground. But the increasingly frequent buffelgrass wildfires are killing these tortoises.[35]

Tamarisk: The Thirsty Invader

Habitat destroyers alter earth, fire, and even water. Tamarisk's superpower is water. With its deep taproot, this woody plant from Eurasia (also known as salt cedar) can guzzle *300 gallons of water per day*, drying up underground springs and rapidly altering stream-flow ecology. It can also increase the amount of salt in soil. The plant excretes salt through its leaves, and when the leaves fall, their salty coating increases the salinity of the surrounding ground.[36]

Originally brought to the United States in the 1800s from Eurasia, tamarisk was used as an ornamental plant, as a possible source of wood production, and as a means of preventing soil erosion. Slow in spreading when first introduced, tamarisk began spreading rapidly in the 1930s, encouraged on by periods of drought, the clearing of native forests, and the construction of dams.[37] Its prolific reproduction—generating more than 500,000 seeds a year—didn't hurt either. Growing about one foot per month, it now covers more than 1.5 million acres in the United States.[38]

Tamarisk poses a major threat to fish species, owing to its ability to drastically change the ecology of streams. The ash meadows speckled dace (a small fish that lives in warm springs and their outflows), the ash meadows Amargosa pupfish (which can occur in spring pools with no more than a half-inch of water), the Rio Grande silvery minnow (one of the most endangered fish species in the United States), and the Arkansas River shiner (a small native minnow that lives in the sandy-bottom streams of the Arkansas River drainage) are just a few of the many fish threatened by Tamarisk.[39]

Purple Loosestrife: The Purple Plague

Commonly called "the purple plague," purple loosestrife is a small flowering plant, native to Eurasia, that has invaded virtually every state in America.[40] It is believed to have come into the United States in the 1800s in the dry ballast of ships. (Ships collected dry material such as soil and rock to use as ballast and then deposited it when they reached their destinations.) Purple loosestrife has also been intentionally introduced—as an ornamental plant, as a pollen source for honey producers, and for medical purposes.[41]

Blooming from June to September, the purple plague is aggressive and adaptable. It commonly produces thirty or more flower stems, which, in the course of a season, have the capacity to produce *millions of seeds*. As if this weren't bad enough, it can also spread through ground shoots, averaging a growth rate of one foot per year.[42]

Purple loosestrife compromises the survival of many endangered and threatened species by altering their habitats. One species at a particular disadvantage is the petite bog turtle—considered one of the rarest freshwater turtles in the United States.[43] It requires wetlands with shallow water and open areas. But when purple loosestrife enters the scene, it dries up the wetlands and leaves a dense outcrop of itself. This thick stand of purple plague is hard for the bog turtle to move in. Losing a preferred habitat, it eventually disappears from purple loosestrife–infested wetlands. Bog turtles aren't the only endangered species that suffer. By altering the landscape, purple loosestrife also harms sandhill cranes and endangered salmon in the Pacific Northwest.[44]

A Special Case: Pacific Salmon

Pacific salmon constitute a special case study, because they are threatened by a number of invasive species—plants, snails, and fish.[45] In the first of these categories is purple loosestrife, which replaces the cattails and sedges along riverbanks that provide food for juvenile salmon. The juvenile salmon feed on the material from decaying riverbank plants in the spring and winter, but purple loosestrife decays on a fall schedule, decreasing the food supply. In addition, the Eurasian water milfoil, an invasive aquatic plant that arrived in the United States in the ballasts of ships, alters the dissolved oxygen content of the water.

Then there is the New Zealand mud snail, a creature so small it can fit on the tip of a pin. Yet this tiny invasive can reproduce very quickly, easily covering a one-square-meter area with over 500,000 individuals. The snails compete against the salmon for insect larvae, resulting in less food and poorer nutrition for the latter.

Finally, as juveniles, Pacific salmon must elude introduced predator or competitor fish species as they progress toward the ocean. (A) American shad migrated into the Pacific Northwest in 1871 shortly after being stocked in the Sacramento River in California. The shad are thought to reduce the salmon's food source—namely, plankton. (B) Brook trout entered the Pacific Northwest in 1913, with the opening of the first commercial hatchery. Primarily identified as a threat to native bull and cutthroat trout, they've recently been shown to decrease juvenile salmon populations. And (C) the introduced channel catfish can grow to more than two feet in length. These predators feed primarily on juvenile salmon.

Pacific salmon already face a whole host of threats to their survival. A migrating species, they are blocked by hydroelectric dams to and from their spawning grounds. They also require cold and well-oxygenated water and are harmed when their waters are diverted for other purposes, such as agriculture. The addition of so many invasive species to their already numerous threats makes their survival much more uncertain.

A TROUBLED FUTURE

Invasive species have become a force to be reckoned with throughout the United States. The mighty fire ants, the burning buffelgrass, the multiplying zebra mussels—these and other invasives are bringing about consequences we never imagined or anticipated. No longer limited to a few outlying coastal areas, they have now affected the entire country. They can be found on more than 100 million acres, and our most vulnerable species are suffering for it.[46]

Even "protected" endangered-species habitats are in grave danger. National wildlife refuges provide some of the most valuable habitat for endangered wildlife. In fact, nearly 60 refuges were created for the express purpose of protecting endangered species.[47] Today, however, the number one threat to refuges themselves is invasive species. The national parks are similarly valuable, providing a home for nearly 400 endangered and threatened species, but the parks are threatened by 6,500 invasive species.

Endangered species have already taken quite a beating. We've reduced their numbers, destroyed their habitats, and introduced competitors. To get back on their feet, they'll need our help. By discontinuing the introduction of invasive species and instead caring for our *native* plants and wildlife, we can give endangered species a better shot at survival. In this way, we won't just be giving endangered species a chance, we'll be giving ourselves the opportunity to live in a world rich with a beautiful diversity.

The Fungus Amongus— Toad as Victim

CHAD PEELING

Chad Peeling grew up at the zoological park founded by his father and spent his formative years exploring this unusual backyard. His interest in herpetology erupted early and he was handling crocodiles and snakes before he could drive. He graduated from Susquehanna University with a self-designed major in zoo management and is now operations manager for Reptiland, a family-owned zoo in Pennsylvania accredited by the Association of Zoos and Aquariums (AZA).

Peeling has delivered more than two thousand lectures about wildlife, science, and conservation and has appeared in several television documentaries. He has written and produced natural history programs about tropical rainforests, biodiversity, coprolites, gecko adhesion, and the global amphibian crisis. Peeling is an active member of the zoological community and serves on steering committees for the AZA Taxon Advisory Groups, which organize cooperative conservation programs among North American zoos.

As a principal in Peeling Productions, a spin-off exhibit fabrication firm, Peeling participates in the design and production of large-scale traveling exhibitions that tour North American zoos, museums, and aquariums. Exhibitions from the Peeling Productions fleet have been hosted by the American Museum of Natural History, the National Geographic Society, the San Diego Zoo, and dozens of other preeminent institutions. Peeling travels regularly and is a passionate advocate for science literacy and personal environmental responsibility.

In "The Fungus Amongus"—the first of two chapters in this book by Chad Peeling—we discover a different side of the cane toad story: the reality that not all amphibians are ultra-successful invaders like the cane toad. In fact, far more frogs and toads are currently threatened—many of them, ironically, by other species that have invaded their own habitats.

Every evening from March to May, just before dusk, I fight a war I know I will never win. I launch a barrage of pyrotechnic noisemakers into the air at my family's zoological park in Pennsylvania in an attempt to scare off enormous flocks of migrating starlings that roost in trees and blanket the grounds in filthy guano. The flocks peel away briefly after each shot, but quickly resume formation and descend again in a relentless assault that lasts until full darkness. If I expend forty to sixty rounds and an hour of my life, I can cut the evening's landing party down to a few hundred birds; if I don't, the trees will seethe with tens of thousands.

Starlings are European birds that don't belong in North America. They were deliberately released in New York City around the turn of the twentieth century by a well-intentioned literary aficionado who wanted to seed the New World with creatures mentioned in the works of Shakespeare. Originally numbering about one hundred, the birds released in the 1890s have multiplied and spread themselves over the continent in a plaguelike infestation. Some researchers estimate the current North American population of starlings at more than 150 million. Their flocks blacken the skies, foul public parks, compete with native songbirds, and may even act as disease vectors.

When rogue species take hold on this scale, it is impossible to bring them under control. The war is unwinnable.

No wonder I don't like starlings.

●— ●— ●—

Like weeds, rogue species are defined by the context in which we find them. In their native lands, most are charming members of the natural cacophony. They evolved with a suite of other organisms—predators, prey, competitors, and parasites—that keep their populations in check. But extracted from those constraints and released in new territory, a species may become an environmental disaster. Of course, not all species are capable of thriving in a new environment, and it's impossible to predict which will become ensconced in a given ecosystem, let alone come to dominate the new territories in which they find themselves. Who would have thought that a European songbird could take over North America—or that a toad could wreak havoc on Australia?

Most people live among rogue species without noticing them. Within a bicycle ride of my home in Pennsylvania, one can experience the consequences of multiple invasions. Wetlands are carpeted in purple loosestrife, an invasive plant that out-competes dozens of native species. Tender leaves and flowers are skeletonized by clusters of Japanese beetles. Foreign diseases and parasites are erasing entire tree species—American elms, American chestnuts, hemlocks—and reordering the forest mosaic. And every few summers, the verdant Appalachian Mountains turn brown with gypsy moth damage.

In warmer climates invasive species pose an even bigger threat, because a greater variety of invaders can survive in the absence of killing frost. Within the United States, South Florida is the extreme example. The area around Miami has become a melting pot of escaped creatures, including South American parrots, Old World pythons, Asian fish, African monkeys, and, yes, cane toads.

Ironically, even as one member of an animal group becomes invasive, others in the same group may become victims of invasion. The irony is particularly bitter in the case of amphibians, the animal group made up of frogs (including toads), salamanders, and the legless caecilians. While a few species of frogs have gone rogue—American bullfrogs west of the Rockies, African clawed frogs in warm parts of North America, and, of course, cane toads throughout the tropics and subtropics—a startling percentage of the world's amphibian species appear to be in rapid decline. It is estimated that a third of the 6,500 described species are threatened with extinction, making amphibians the most endangered class of vertebrate animals—and some say even this figure is too conservative.

Habitat destruction, over-collection for food and the pet trade, pollution, and climate change all take a hefty toll on amphibians. But the most alarming threat is a rogue species of soil fungus that infects their skin and spreads like wildfire. The disease it causes is called chytridiomycosis.

Rogue species come in many shapes and sizes. The amphibian chytrid fungus is tiny. A single microscopic spore is enough to infect a pristine habitat. Amphibians breathe and absorb water through their skin, which is thin and moist. Like a giant exterior lung, the skin is an organ that exchanges chemicals—good and bad—with its surroundings. But it's also perfect for growing infections. The amphibian chytrid fungus (*Batrachochytrium dendrobatidis*) thrives in the cool, moist habitats preferred by most amphibians and quickly colonizes the skin of exposed animals. Amphibian skin thickens in response to the fungus, which is why the infection kills so quickly—thick skin can't exchange gasses or absorb water efficiently. The animals asphyxiate and dehydrate.

Dead and dying frogs have been found in huge numbers after chytrid was introduced to their environment, and the disease has now reached every continent where amphibians live. Although it is easily treated in captivity by soaking the animals in glorified athlete's foot medication, there is no remedy in sight for wild populations.

One particularly well-documented area, near El Cope, Panama, was among the most diverse amphibian habitats on the planet until chytrid arrived in 2004. Within six months of the disease's arrival, 90 percent of the amphibians in the region were dead. And El Cope is not an isolated case. A similar epidemic is at work in parts of Australia, Africa, Europe, and the United States. If current trends continue, we may lose a substantial percentage of the world's amphibian diversity in the foreseeable future—an extinction event greater than any in human history.

Like any rogue species, the amphibian chytrid fungus poses a problem only because it's on the loose. There is good evidence that particular strains of the fungus originated in Asia (and possibly other continents) as harmless members of the ecosystem. Moving strains from one area to another is what touched off the epidemic. The fungus may originally have been distributed in African clawed frogs, which have been shipped to laboratories far and wide since the 1930s. American bullfrogs and other laboratory species are now carriers as well. Labs may have spread the fungus in wastewater or by releasing frogs directly into local waterways. (Clawed frogs, themselves, have become rogue species in some parts of North America.)

Whatever the original point of infection, the amphibian chytrid fungus is spreading—probably on the feet of birds, insects, researchers, and tourists. Field biologists are tracking the leading edge of the disease as it marches across continents. In its wake the fungus leaves silent forests where choruses of frogs once called. To add insult to injury, the invasive cane toads appear to be far less susceptible to chytrid than other amphibians.

The prospects for many amphibians are downright depressing, but there is a glimmer of hope in the response inspired by this epidemic. Widespread media coverage and a spate of new conservation and research projects have brought the plight of amphibians to a global audience. Academic researchers are racing to catalogue the full breadth of amphibian diversity before it's gone. Field biologists are exploring the ecological impact of losing a whole category of organisms from the middle of the food web. Conservation biologists are scrambling for ways to slow or stop the die-offs, and international organizations have been created to help coordinate a global response. In short, the crisis has the attention of some of the brightest minds in science.

Desperate to salvage amphibian species from the invasive fungus, zoos, museums, and academic institutions have begun to establish assurance colonies of endangered frogs in captivity. Captive colonies do not offer long-term salvation for a species, but at least they hedge against immediate extinction and buy time for creative solutions.

One promising approach, being undertaken near Melbourne, Australia, is to drive the evolution of chytrid resistance. Researchers have released hundreds of captive-born frogs into habitats where their species was previously wiped out by the epidemic. The fungus remains in the environment and most of the released frogs succumb to the infection. But some have survived, apparently resistant to the fungus. These survivors may pass their genes to the next generation and found a new, resistant population. Releasing huge numbers of offspring into an infected environment is like trying to beat the lottery by buying lots of tickets. It increases the odds of introducing a protective gene to the population, and lets natural selection do the rest.

On a recent trip to Australia, I strolled by an open-air restaurant that advertised "World Famous Cane Toad Races." As a zoo herpetologist—one who popularizes the science of reptiles and amphibians—I couldn't resist.

After dinner a crowd gathered and a top-hat-wearing emcee began picking contestants who came forward to select their "racers" from a gaggle of large toads, each with a white number on its back. At the start of the race, toads were released from under a bucket at the center of a ring and the first toad to reach the outer edge was the winner. The event was silly, but the emcee's running commentary was hilarious and the audience reactions were fascinating. Most of the human contestants were foreign tourists who treated the toads as charming, if slightly gross. But the Australian contestants, overrun by cane toads for decades, clearly disliked them, feigning attempts to squish the toads at every chance. I've kept and cared for cane toads in captivity for decades and it's hard for me to imagine anyone wanting to squish one—soft-bodied, toothless, posing no real threat to humans.

I fully understand wanting to kill foul-smelling songbirds—but who would want to kill a toad? I guess living with the consequences of an invasive species can make a person dislike almost anything.

Hawaii

Paradise Lost

Daniel Simberloff

Daniel Simberloff is a biologist at the University of Tennessee, Knoxville, where he has been the Nancy Gore Hunger Professor of Environmental Studies since his arrival in 1997. His A.B. and Ph.D. degrees are from Harvard University.

Simberloff's research in ecology, evolution, and biogeography focuses particularly on which species coexist (or fail to do so) in biological communities and the mechanisms permitting or forbidding coexistence. For the past twenty-five years, this focus has led him to explore invasions by non-native species, including geographic patterns of invasions, impacts of invasive species, and evolution of invaders and native species in response to their coexistence. His five hundred publications on these and related topics include the books *Ecological Communities: Conceptual Issues and the Evidence* (Princeton University Press, 1984; co-edited with D. R. Strong, Jr., L. G. Abele, and A. B. Thistle) and *Strangers in Paradise: Impact and Management of Non-Indigenous Species in Florida* (Island Press, 1997; co-edited with D. C. Schmitz and T. C. Brown). Simberloff is also editor-in-chief of the journal *Biological Invasions* (Springer) and senior editor of the forthcoming *Encyclopedia of Biological Invasions* (University of California Press).

In "Hawaii: Paradise Lost," Simberloff explores the remarkable story of one of the world's most remote inhabited island chains, an archipelago that many assume includes significant pockets of pristine nature unaltered by human impact. Not so. In fact, as Simberloff shows, the Hawaii we visit today has little in common with the "real" Hawaii that the Polynesians first discovered centuries ago.

BEFORE THE FALL

There have been Hawaiian Islands for at least 70 million years, but most of them are long gone. The existing Hawaiian Islands are young in geological terms: The oldest main island, Kauai, rose from the sea only about 5 million years ago, and the youngest, Hawaii, less than 700,000 years ago. The entire archipelago rides northwesterly at a leisurely thirty-two miles per million years on the geological Pacific plate. As the plate passes over a volcanic hotspot, the islands are pushed up. Over millions of years, they rise above the surface of the ocean to great heights, gradually wear down and fall beneath the surface, while new ones rise to the southeast to replace them.[1]

The islands of this archipelago are among the most isolated on earth; they have never been much closer to North America or Asia than they are today. Until recently, the resident plants and animals reflected this isolation, with most native species evolving in the archipelago and restricted to it. The results of this process were remarkable and amazing.

For example, Hawaii has about 2,000 native plants, descended from about 275 ancestral species that somehow reached the islands from continents thousands of miles away. Hawaii originally lacked many large groups of plants; there were no gymnosperms, no mangroves, and only one genus of palms. However, the relatively few plants that did reach these isolated islands evolved and split into strange and beautiful species. The silverswords, for example, are a group of thirty-one species of often striking, swordlike shrubs and small trees found only in the Hawaiian Islands.[2]

Similarly, only half of all insect orders in the world are native to Hawaii, yet of about 2,000 species of fruit flies, about 40 percent are found only in this archipelago. Probably just one or at most two ancestral fly species arrived on an older island that is now submerged, and the occasional movement of individuals among the islands, which are themselves many miles apart, followed by the evolution of these isolated populations led to the explosion of diversity now evident.[3]

Another example: Hawaii has about 750 species of land snails, derived from 22 to 24 independent colonizations; almost all are endemic to Hawaii.[4]

Hawaiian native birds arose from about 20 separate successful immigrations, mostly of species associated with water, with hundreds of thousands of years passing between arrivals of new species in the archipelago. Over 80 percent of native Hawaiian birds are found nowhere else.[5] The most remarkable Hawaiian bird group is an endemic family or subfamily called honeycreepers, descendants of a single ancestral seed-eating finch species from South America that found its way to Kauai (then the youngest and largest island) between 3 and 4 million years ago and radiated into more than 56 species (of which 23 exist today) that fill ecological niches that other seedeaters as well as insect- and nectar-feeding birds would occupy on continents.[6]

Scientists refer to the peculiar composition of the Hawaiian flora and fauna—the absence of entire major groups, the evolutionary radiation of others to take their place—as *disharmony*. The long isolation from humans (and other species) as well as the disharmonious biota left Hawaii supremely vulnerable to certain kinds of alien species: There were no native mammals but a bat and a seal, hence no carnivores or rats; there were no ants, no worms, no mosquitoes. Many birds were flightless; plants lacked thorns. Many pathogens common on continents were completely absent, so the native species had not evolved resistance to them. Having evolved in the absence of various potential enemies, Hawaiian native species were ill-equipped to deal with them if they were to arrive.

Here was a disaster waiting to happen.

Humans Arrive—
With Their Guests

This evolutionary Eden began crumbling long before Captain Cook's arrival opened the Hawaiian Islands to European settlement. Polynesians arrived between 600 and 800 A.D., and by 1600 A.D. Polynesians and the species they brought with them had greatly changed at least 80 percent of all the Hawaiian lands below 1,500 feet in elevation.

According to the traditional explanation for this change, fires were set to clear land for agriculture and for other purposes.[7] However, recent evidence points to another primary cause: Pacific rats (*Rattus exulans*), hitchhiking with the Polynesians throughout the Pacific, arrived by at least 1000 A.D. and quickly destroyed extensive lowland palm forests by gnawing on their seeds. Many native bird species, adapted to the forest habitat, disappeared as the forest was replaced by grasses and shrubs—in some parts of Hawaii, well before Polynesians established settlements.[8]

Polynesians also brought pigs, whose rooting transformed much habitat, and the Polynesians themselves hunted. All of these factors contributed to a hecatomb of bird extinction. Most of the lost species are known only from fossils. Among them were flightless geese, ibises, and rails, a hawk, three owls, and two crows. Most of the thirty-odd honeycreepers that are now extinct disappeared between the arrival of the Polynesians and that of Europeans.[9]

But the changes wrought by the Polynesians were just the beginning. The arrival of Europeans, beginning with Captain Cook in 1778, then of Americans and Asians, led to a flood of invading plants, animals, and pathogens that have utterly transformed the entire Hawaiian landscape. Often these interlopers interact in ways that exacerbate their individual impacts, a process known as *invasional meltdown*.

Here's a simple example. Hawaii had no native mosquitoes, but several species quickly followed the Europeans. Five species of biting mosquitoes are now present—including the yellow fever mosquito and the Asian tiger mosquito—but probably the most consequential is the southern house mosquito (*Culex quinquefasciatus*), inadvertently introduced from Mexico in 1826 in water casks on a whaling ship. It is widespread up to about 4,000 feet in elevation in all Hawaiian habitats and is active at night, tormenting anyone trying to sleep unprotected. Its major ecological impact did not appear until the first half of the twentieth century.

At that time, many songbirds from all over the world (but especially Asia) were introduced into Hawaii as amenities or escaped pets. Some of these birds carried avian malaria (a plasmodium related to the pathogen that causes human malaria) and avian pox, a virus. The introduced bird species, having coexisted and coevolved with these pathogens for eons, were resistant to them, but the native Hawaiian birds, having evolved in isolation for several million years, were devastated by the new diseases. For instance, for some native Hawaiian bird species, 65–90 percent of individuals die after one bite from a mosquito vectoring the malaria plasmodium.[10]

Many other factors have also contributed to the decline of native Hawaiian birds. Of 114 endemic species known (new fossil species are still being discovered), 66 are now extinct. We have already seen that Pacific rats unwittingly introduced by Polynesians caused many bird species to go extinct well before Europeans arrived. However, the boat traffic and settlement that followed Captain Cook were at least as catastrophic. Of 38 native Hawaiian forest bird species that existed when European colonization began, 14 are already extinct and 15 are basket cases on the federal Endangered Species List.[11]

Avian pox and malaria contribute mightily, but the main reason is habitat destruction, especially of native forest. The problem is that most lowland areas have been cleared for agriculture and other human development, so most remaining native forest, the normal habitat of most of these species, is in very high elevations to which these birds are not well adapted. Those few substantial areas of lower-elevation native forest that remain are unavailable to the birds because they are mosquito-ridden and have many resistant introduced birds that act as reservoirs for the malaria and pox. The only glimmer of hope is that one native Hawaiian species—the amakihi (*Hemignathus virens*)—has evolved substantial resistance to avian malaria in just the last few years.[12]

So it's highly ironic that Hawaii is known as a bird-lovers' paradise. Most visitors see no native species except for a few waterbirds, because the remaining native land birds are mostly rare and largely restricted to high mountain habitats. Nevertheless, a birdwatcher wandering in lowland suburban areas—for instance, the campus of the University of Hawaii at Manoa—can easily see birds from Asia, Europe, Africa, and North and South America in a single afternoon. Most of the fifty-three established exotic bird species came in the first half of the nineteenth century. Many were introduced simply to establish reminders of home for new settlers. The Hui Manu (Hawaiian for "Bird Society") was organized specifically to augment the songbirds of the islands and brought, among many other species, cardinals and northern mockingbirds from North America and white-rumped shamas from India. The Honolulu Mejiro Club, named for the Japanese white-eye (introduced by the Hawaii Territorial Board of Agriculture in 1929 to control pest insects) had as its raison d'être the introduction of other Japanese birds (bush warblers, for example).[13] Other exotic birds are cage escapes or releases (e.g., red-vented bulbul, mitred conure) or were introduced as game animals (e.g., mallard, Kalij pheasant). Some, such as the white-eye, Asian myna, and African cattle egret, were released in attempts to manage insect populations through a process known as *biological control.*

Aside from vectoring diseases that ravage native birds, introduced birds have participated in several invasional meltdowns. Notably, mynas disperse seeds of *Lantana camara*, a South American weed that dominates vast areas of pastureland, while white-eyes are the main disperser of seeds of firetree, a tree of Atlantic islands that is transforming entire ecosystems—especially on the Big Island of Hawaii, as will be described below.

Other impacts of introduced birds can be extremely subtle and, though not ecosystem-wide, devastating to particular species. For example, the North American mallard was introduced around 1900 for hunting, and it hybridizes with the native koloa duck. On Oahu and Maui, there are no purebred koloas left, and populations on the other islands are threatened with a similar fate.[14]

Although the Hawaiian Islands have only two native mammal species (a bat and a seal), nineteen introduced mammal species have established populations, and three of these are predators that ravage native birds. Housecats became feral soon after the arrival of Europeans and feast on birds; Oahu alone was recently estimated to contain at least 80,000 feral cats. The Asian roof or ship rat probably arrived as a stowaway on European ships between 1870 and 1880. Like cats, ship rats are excellent climbers, and in addition to devouring birds and their eggs they damage sugar cane and various stored foods. The small Indian mongoose was deliberately introduced in 1882 to control rats in sugar cane fields, but it also feeds on native ground-nesting birds (such as the Hawaiian goose and seabirds) and insects. Its impact on rats is limited because the mongoose forages only in the day and the rats are active at night.[15]

Although animals such as cats and mongooses have huge impacts on particular native species, introduced plants are more commonly the invaders that can transform entire ecosystems.

African molasses grass and tropical American bush beardgrass invaded seasonal lower-elevation woodlands on the Big Island beginning in the late 1960s. Before then, grass ground cover in these woodlands was sparse and fire rare. Now the grasses are rampant between the trees and shrubs and grow into their canopies. Fire frequency has more than doubled, and the extent of each fire is much greater. Native plants are killed, but the exotic grasses recover quickly and produce dense masses of highly flammable fuel. Each successive fire kills more of the native vegetation and this positive feedback loop has changed a native-dominated woodland into an alien-dominated grassland. Other introduced grasses have wrought similar transformations in other parts of the archipelago.[16]

Such invasions have further ecosystem consequences. For example, spread of molasses grass leads to much greater soil nitrogen concentrations and greater uptake of nitrogenous substances by plants. Because most native Hawaiian plants are adapted to thrive in the nutrient-poor volcanic soil, and many introduced species require higher concentrations of nutrients (including nitrogen), the spread of molasses grass can facilitate invasion by other aliens in an invasional meltdown.

The firetree from the Canary Islands, intentionally introduced in the early twentieth century as an ornamental, was widely planted by the Hawaii Department of Forestry for erosion control and has spread with surprising consequences. It is a nitrogen-fixer, and it is invading nitrogen-poor volcanic soils. The firetree is replacing the native 'ohi'a lehua tree, and the nitrogen and water content of the canopy of the new forest is approximately double that of the original one.[17] As just noted, many exotic ornamentals have been unable to invade natural areas because they are not adapted to the low nutrient levels, and now firetree is fertilizing the soil and removing this barrier.

This meltdown has other components. Hawaii had no native earthworms, but several exotic species are now present. The density of earthworms beneath firetree is much greater than that under ʻohiʻa lehua, and the worms are helping to bury the nitrogen-rich fallen firetree leaves in the soil, thereby increasing rates of nitrogen-cycling and exacerbating the transformation to a system coming to be dominated by exotic plants.[18] Further, the main seed disperser of firetree is the Japanese white-eye, with introduced pigs playing a secondary role. Thus, many introduced species are combining with firetree to produce a rapidly advancing invasive juggernaut.

Many other introduced plants dominate parts of the Hawaiian landscape. The archipelago has about 1,200 native plant species, but Polynesians and especially Western visitors and colonists have brought more than 10,000 exotic plants, of which about 1,100 are established outside of cultivation.[19] Miconia, or velvet-leaf tree, was deliberately introduced from tropical and subtropical America in the 1960s and was first reported as spreading in 1982. Because over 60 percent of Tahiti is now dominated by miconia, this invasion of Hawaii raised alarms even as the tree was being sold in nurseries. The outcome of an eradication campaign launched in 1991 remains to be determined. Miconia tends to crowd out and overgrow native plants, and its shallow root system does not hold soil well, leading to erosion and landslides.

Clidemia, also known as Koster's curse, was introduced from the American tropics and first found on Oahu in 1941. It has spread to other islands, forms monocultures on the forest floor, and crowds out native species in disturbed areas, especially in moist forest areas. Brazilian strawberry guava was deliberately introduced for fruit in 1825 and now occupies hundreds of thousands of acres. It occupies habitats similar to those of clidemia, and its germination is facilitated by trampling by wild pigs.

Strawberry guava releases toxins into the soil that inhibit native plants, and it also is a refuge for two alien fruit flies that cost Hawaiian agriculture millions of dollars annually.[20]

Even the intertidal coast is not immune to plant invasions. Beginning in 1902, several mangrove species were deliberately introduced to the Hawaiian Islands, dramatically changing parts of the coastline. Before European and Asian colonization, intertidal wetlands were mainly occupied by algae and fungi along with a few herbs and small shrubs. Europeans and Asians first introduced small plants that came to dominate much of the intertidal, such as saltwort from southern North America and Central and South America and seashore paspalum, a grass of unknown origin. Small hibiscus trees, also introduced, may have existed in the highest intertidal. Many of these sites are now mangrove forests dominated by tall red mangrove from Florida, some of which also have Asian large-leafed mangrove as a midstory, with few or no groundcover plants. Mangrove forests drop over 18,000 pounds of leaves per year per acre, while the roots accumulate sediment and form critical habitat for fishes and invertebrates. The entire high intertidal ecosystem has been utterly transformed.[21]

Much less conspicuous organisms than trees and fire-enhancing grasses have drastically changed components of Hawaiian ecosystems. Ants are the most harmful insects in Hawaii, and all forty-three species are introduced. The African big-headed ant, an accidental nineteenth-century import, is a ferocious predator implicated in the decline and extinction of many native insects and possibly snails. It has also formed a new mutualism with a terrible agricultural pest (also introduced)—the pink pineapple mealybug, yet another example of invasional meltdown. The Argentine ant, accidentally introduced in 1940, quickly became enormously numerous at upper elevations. Aside from delivering a painful bite, this species kills predators of introduced scale insects that are agricultural and horticultural pests, and it kills many native moths and bees (some of which pollinate native plants). It is found as high as 9,200 feet on Maui, and in some areas almost no native insects survive its advance.[22]

More than twenty species of introduced snails have established populations in Hawaii, several with huge impacts. The giant African snail was introduced in 1936 as a food item, though it has never found culinary favor. It is a huge snail and reaches great numbers in fields and gardens, requiring massive use of snail bait. It is herbivorous and may threaten some native plants. The predaceous rosy wolf snail from the southeastern United States was introduced in 1955 in a failed attempt to control the giant African snail (adults of which are simply too large to serve as prey). The rosy wolf snail has, however, preyed heavily on endemic Hawaiian land and tree snails. For example, populations of the beautiful and endangered Oahu tree snail disappeared suddenly from a mountain where they were being studied exactly when the rosy wolf snail arrived in this area.[23]

Introduced species can be terrible nuisances even when they do not threaten native species or agriculture. Five introduced frogs, plus the cane toad, have established populations in the Hawaiian Islands. The cane toad was introduced in 1932, just as it was in Australia, to control insects in sugar cane fields, and it failed in Hawaii just as resoundingly and with many of the same unintended impacts. The Caribbean coqui, introduced into Maui in the late 1980s and later into the Big Island, is a less fearsome but much noisier frog. Its nightly bell-like call keeps people awake and on Maui has led to a decline in hotel occupancy simply because of the annoyance. The coquis achieve great numbers on Maui, where they devour enormous quantities of insects, potentially depriving native birds of prey, and themselves serve as a prey base to increase rat and mongoose populations.

It's Not Over

Hawaii faces several threats of future invaders whose impacts could rival the worst of those already there. Three stand out.

The brown tree snake from the Admiralty Islands near New Guinea has already devastated the birds of Guam, extinguishing nine native species since its arrival after World War II and leaving a silent forest. In addition, it has caused millions of dollars of electrical damage each year by draping itself over wires and causing short-circuits. To make matters worse, it eats poultry and pets and enters homes at night, biting children. Single individuals of the brown tree snake have already reached Hawaii at least ten times, at both Honolulu International Airport and adjacent Hickam Air Force Base, arriving on planes from Guam in either wheel wells or cargo. Each time they have been destroyed on the runway, and extraordinary measures are undertaken on Guam to prevent their access to the airport. However, the threat remains, and if the snake were to establish itself in Hawaii it could easily sound the death knell for several of the already endangered native birds.[24]

The infamous South American imported red fire ant is widely established in the southern United States, more recently in California and Queensland, Australia. Wherever it is established, it is a staggering pest, through its painful stings, impacts on agriculture, and destruction of native insects and other animals. Individual queens and small colonies could easily arrive in Hawaii in various kinds of commercial or military cargo.

Finally, South American Siam weed is a huge pest of agricultural as well as pristine natural habitats in Australia, Asia, and Africa, and it could easily reach Hawaii through small seeds in agricultural products or packing material. As with the imported red fire ant, there is no reason to believe that this species could not colonize almost all areas of the Hawaiian Islands except for high elevations.[25]

WHAT TO DO?

The best solution to the introduced-species problem is to keep them out in the first place. It is too late to keep out the hundreds of species that are already established, but vigilance can help to prevent new ones like the red fire ant or brown tree snake from arriving. Anyone arriving at Honolulu International Airport finds sniffer dogs waiting in the baggage claim area, one of the last lines of defense after publicity on the plane and warnings in the customs and immigration area about bringing in unprocessed fruit and vegetables, animals, and dirt that may carry seeds or mites or microbes. In fact, specific quarantine and exclusion programs of the U.S. Department of Agriculture, the Hawaii Department of Agriculture, the Hawaii Department of Land and Natural Resources, and the U.S. Fish and Wildlife Service allow authorities to seize many species as well as the goods carrying them and in some instances to penalize the persons transporting them.[26]

Hawaii has also established an Invasive Species Council and has imposed fees on incoming freight shipments to pay for invasive species inspection, quarantine, and eradication, while pending legislation imposes penalties of at least $100,000 per violation on "[a]ny person or organization who intentionally imports, possesses, harbors, or transports . . . any prohibited or restricted plant, animal, or microorganism without a permit, with intent to propagate, sell, or release that plant, animal, or microorganism."[27]

However, as is also apparent to anyone arriving at the airport, these efforts are underfunded and understaffed, and someone determined to bring in individuals of some species, especially small ones, could probably easily do it. For that matter, it would often be a straightforward matter to send an invader (say, seeds of a potentially invasive plant) through first-class mail. In addition, some unintended introductions hitchhike by various means—in shipping containers, wooden pallets, ceramic tiles, cars, machinery, and the like. Substantially stemming the flow of invaders into Hawaii is certainly possible but will require even greater commitment of resources.

Hawaii has also engaged both its citizens and visitors through a highly visible education campaign about the costs of invasive species, and the long history of damaging invasions means that news media report invasive species stories more frequently and prominently than anywhere else other than possibly New Zealand. It is unlikely that any Hawaiian citizen does not know about the threat posed by the brown tree snake, while the noisy controversy surrounding the recent proposal to establish a large commercial ferry between the main Hawaiian Islands featured concerns that such a vessel would inevitably lead to the mongoose colonizing Kauai, the only island it has not reached. The state has established hotlines where citizens can report sightings of invasions.

Certainly the heightened awareness of the invasive species issue in Hawaii has led to a more educated and vigilant citizenry, and organized activities (such as volunteer removal projects for exotic weeds) have partly compensated for inadequate state and federal funding. Ad hoc actions by engaged, enraged citizens also contribute. I have seen cars screech to a halt in remote parts of the Big Island so their occupants could run out and rip up miconia plants visible from the road.

However, introduced species are a particularly insidious problem, because a very few individuals (or a single seed or pregnant female) can initiate an invasion, and an initial population can remain unseen until is has spread so far that eradication is difficult or impossible. Several of Hawaii's most invasive species were, in fact, detected early enough that they probably could have been eradicated easily. For example, clidemia was discovered in 1941 while restricted to a few acres and for a decade did not spread beyond 200 acres, before suddenly and rapidly spreading across the landscape; it now infests over 200,000 acres and is on all the main islands. However, no actions were taken to control it until 1954, by which time it was too late. The threat was recognized early, but authorities failed to act because of a false sense of security: A thrips that feeds on clidemia had controlled an invasion of this plant in Fiji and it was assumed that the same insect, if introduced to Hawaii, would thrive as a biological control agent. When finally introduced, the thrips was a miserable failure.[28]

Another difficulty with controlling invasions is that a single person can defeat an eradication attempt by carrying out rogue introductions of the target species, and a well-mobilized and vocal group, even if small, can even prevent an eradication or management project from getting under way. A potential biological control project for strawberry guava entailing the introduction of a Brazilian scale insect that eats it (and no other plant species found in Hawaii) has long been stymied by a "Save the Guava" campaign, replete with rallies and an online petition, mounted by a group of citizens who happen to like the tree, invasive or not.[29] Even the annoying coqui frog has its advocates. Although the public was overwhelmingly ready to do anything to get rid of this loud nuisance, a government official motivated by animal rights concerns delayed management operations for a year.[30]

Perhaps the most controversial management issue regarding an invader in Hawaii is the attempt to reduce the population of feral pigs, descendants of a British pair released by Captain Cook and supplemented later by additional European pigs, as well as a smaller variety brought by the Polynesians a thousand years earlier. The two varieties hybridized and their progeny are among the most widespread and destructive of all invaders in the archipelago, affecting almost all plant communities. Their rooting, to find soil animals (especially introduced earthworms) and starchy roots, leads to erosion and facilitates invasion by exotic plants, whose seeds they ingest and then deposit in excrement. They favor strawberry guava and firetree in particular and are credited with greatly advancing the invasions of those two species. The ditches they dig and wallow in become breeding grounds for mosquitoes carrying avian pox and malaria. Their favorite foods include a number of native plant species (such as tree ferns and lobeliads), some of them already threatened.[31]

A program by the Nature Conservancy in the 1990s to lower pig densities by snaring in montane nature reserves engendered heated opposition from an unholy alliance of native hunters and animal rights advocates. The hunters descend from the original Polynesians who have hunted pigs for a millennium, and they see pigs as not only a traditional food but a major source of protein. The animal rights advocates, such as People for the Ethical Treatment of Animals, are primarily vegetarians and usually no friends of hunters, but they objected to the snares as a particularly cruel lethal tool. The holy grail of animal rights advocates is some sort of contraceptive bait to manage invasive mammals, but this tool does not exist, the snares were effective, and without management the pigs are contributing to the destruction of forests and the extinction of species. State and federal land managers have also fenced off increasingly large tracts of valuable forest land to exclude pigs, hunting and trapping the animals inside the fence. This procedure, though more effective, is also much more expensive than the snares, and the pro-pig forces are equally opposed to it.[32]

The prospects for preserving what little is left of pre-European Hawaii, much less restoring tracts of agricultural and pasture land to some earlier condition, are dim. Many native species are already extinct, even if some of the chief invaders could be eradicated or at least controlled at much lower levels. Technologies to manage invasive species are numerous.[33] Although the use of introduced biological control agents has in some instances done more harm than good (in Hawaii, the small Indian mongoose, the rosy wolf snail, and the cane toad were all deliberately introduced to control other invaders), a maturing science and much more extensive pre-introduction testing would probably prevent such a disaster today. There have also been many successful management projects using chemical baits, pesticides, and herbicides.

Even brute-force physical methods are sometimes remarkably effective. In Hawaii, U.S. Department of Defense contractors have cleared some areas of invasive mangroves with heavy earthmoving equipment,[34] while a raging infestation of sand bur on the outlying island of Laysan was totally eradicated by a combination of hand-pulling and glyphosate herbicide.[35] But all these methods must be tailored to the particular species and site, and some are very expensive. As we have seen, should technologies exist to deal with a particular problem, even really damaging invaders may have advocates. And the sheer number of high-impact invaders in Hawaii combines with the remoteness and rugged terrain of much of the archipelago to increase the costs involved.

The best we can hope for, and even this will take assiduous effort in perpetuity, is to maintain remote, usually small reserves that will allow us to glimpse what paradise might have looked like . . . if we do not look too closely and see a Japanese white-eye perched on a firetree branch.

Our Invaded Oceans

JAMES T. CARLTON

Dr. James T. Carlton is professor of Marine Sciences at Williams College (Williamstown, Massachusetts) and director, Williams-Mystic, the Maritime Studies Program of Williams College and Mystic Seaport (Mystic, Connecticut). He was an undergraduate at the University of California, Berkeley, majoring in paleontology; took his Ph.D. at UC Davis in ecology; and was a postdoctoral scholar at the Woods Hole Oceanographic Institution. His research priorities are global marine bioinvasions (specifically with respect to their ecosystem impacts, dispersal vectors, and management strategies) as well as global marine extinctions in modern times.

Carlton is the founding editor-in-chief of the international journal *Biological Invasions*. He is a 1996 Pew Fellow in the Environment and Conservation, a Fellow of the American Association for the Advancement of Science, a Duke University Scholar, and a Distinguished Research Fellow of the University of California. He was the first scientist ever to be given the U.S. government's "Recognition Award for Significant and Sustained Contributions to the Prevention and Control of Nonindigenous Species in America's Aquatic Ecosystems," which he received in 1999. He was co-chair of the Marine Biodiversity Committee of the National Academy of Sciences, which produced *Understanding Marine Biodiversity: A Research Agenda for the Nation*. And he has testified nine times on invasive species issues before the U.S. Congress (Senate and House subcommittees).

Carlton's research on marine bioinvasions focuses on the waters of the Northwest Atlantic Ocean (from the Bay of Fundy to New Jersey), the Northeast Pacific Ocean (from Alaska to Mexico), the Hawaiian

Islands, and South Africa. He is the editor and an author of the 1,000-page *Light & Smith Manual: Intertidal Invertebrates from Central California to Oregon*, published in 2007 by the University of California Press. Also in 2007 he received the Nelson Bushnell Prize of Williams College for writing and teaching. In September of the same year, the ribbon was cut on the James T. Carlton Marine Science Center, an 8,800-square-foot research and teaching facility in Mystic, Connecticut, named in his honor.

It's easy to assume that the oceans of planet Earth are relatively immune to the problem of invasive species—after all, the waters of the "seven seas" are not separated by impregnable boundaries, so why shouldn't they contain a more or less homogeneous mixture of plant and animal life? In "Our Invaded Oceans," Carlton shows why this is not so and explains how human intervention, intentional and unintentional, is now bringing about the intermingling of aquatic species from around the world for the first time in the history of our planet.

> *Commerce defies every wind, outrides every tempest, and invades every zone.*
> —by George Bancroft (1800–1891),
> inscribed on the Department of Commerce Building,
> Fifteenth Street, Washington, DC

Before humans went to sea, taking with them an unintentional cargo of marine hitchhikers in and on their vessels, the world's oceans were largely isolated from each other. About 65 million years ago, the Earth's continents and ocean basins had settled into approximately their present positions, creating highly isolated regions where the ensuing millions of years produced the unique provincial diversity that, today, draws us to go forth and explore—and expect to see—the exotic biota of the far-flung corners of the Earth.

And then, in the space of just a few hundred years, tens of millions of years of isolation suddenly came to an end on a global scale.

We don't know when humans first successfully crossed broad waters in sailing craft. We do know that islands in the Mediterranean, reachable only by boat or raft, were peopled over 100,000 years ago. Islands of the South Pacific were colonized tens of thousands of years ago. By 1,000 years ago, the Polynesians had reached the Hawaiian archipelago and the Vikings had reached North America, and by the 1300s Chinese explorers were sailing through the Indian Ocean. Yet despite these early episodes, ocean travel remained largely within ocean basins and, often, within regional limits. Globalization was launched in the 1400s and 1500s, when the first European explorers left the known waters of the Atlantic to sail east into the Indian Ocean and west into the Pacific. With these voyages, the great biological realms of the sea began to merge.

THE OCEAN IN MOTION (I): SAILING SHIPS AS FLOATING BIOLOGICAL ISLANDS

When Francis Drake (later Sir Francis) departed England for the Pacific Ocean in December 1577 on his 120-foot (36.5-meter) three-masted galleon *Pelican*, his wooden ship was laden with supplies, guns, and people. Also aboard were a host of nonhuman living creatures. Rats and mice embarked with cargo or made their way up docking lines at night; insects, spiders, and mites came aboard with food stores and personal belongings; and a potentially wide variety of animals and plants were carried accidentally along with the rocks and boulders placed in the *Pelican*'s hold for ballast.

Also aboard, or more properly outboard, was a cross-section of the marine life of Drake's departure harbor of Plymouth on the Devon coast. Fouling and boring organisms were almost certainly part of this menagerie, despite the measures probably taken by the builders of the *Pelican* to protect the ship's hull against them. Fouling—animal and plant growth on a vessel's hull—was known to be capable of cutting a ship's top speed (eight knots or better in the *Pelican*'s case) nearly in half. More dangerous were the organisms that would bore into the *Pelican*'s wooden hull: the shipworms (which are clams, not worms at all) and gribbles (tiny crustaceans) that would be the scourge of wooden ships for centuries to come. Shipworm (*Teredo*, *Lyrodus*, or *Bankia*) larvae settle on exposed wooden planks, burrow deep into the wood, and can turn a ship's hull into a thin honeycomb, sinking the vessel. In the meantime, one-tenth-inch (2.5-millimeter) gribbles (*Limnoria*) were burrowing from the outside in, stripping away layer after layer of the surface wood, until they reached the shipworm galleries, by which time little wood was to be had.

We don't know what steps the builders of the *Pelican* may have taken against these dangers. It is probable that the ship's hull was treated with tar, hair, and thin wooden planks, the latter to act as sacrificial wood for boring organisms and "weeds," timber that would then be replaced during the voyage; she may also have had cast sheet leading on her hull. But anti-fouling paints were centuries away, as was the regular use of iron and steel in constructing ships.

And so the *Pelican* sailed south toward Africa, her hull covered with sponges, hydroids, barnacles and other crustaceans, sea squirts, seaweed (algae), sea anemones, and bryozoans. Already boring into the hull—despite whatever crude treatments there may have been—were shipworms and gribbles; and if these burrowers had gained any headway, a host of smaller, errant organisms, such as crabs and flatworms, lived in their galleries. Nestling in cracks and crevices on the hull were shore isopods and snails. The anchor and anchor chain had hauled up worms and seaweed from the bottom of Plymouth harbor. Plants and their seeds, shore hopper amphipods, insects, and worms were safely packed in the ballast hold.

In short, the flora and fauna of Europe were about to visit the Pacific Ocean.

As the *Pelican* sailed to the Cape Verde Islands, across the Atlantic to what was to be Argentina, and then to the Pacific coasts of South and North America, she also accumulated more species, which colonized the vessel en route. Indeed, a careful examination of her hull by the time Drake reached the mid-Pacific would have revealed her cruise track by virtue of the ship's biological fingerprinting alone. By the time the *Pelican*, now renamed the *Golden Hinde*, returned to England in 1580, having circumnavigated the globe by way of the Indian Ocean and the Cape of Good Hope, Drake had acquired, and shed, hundreds of species of marine plants and animals.

THE OCEAN IN MOTION (II): SHIPS VERSUS OCEAN CURRENTS

Marine life also flows in the sea on ocean currents. In the North Atlantic Ocean, the *Pelican* had captured the Canary Current as it flowed south along the southern European and northwest African coast. The Canary Current would then have been subsumed and entrained by the westward-flowing North Equatorial Current, which collides with the shallow waters of the Caribbean Sea. From here, a number of smaller currents flow through and around eastern North and Central America, some of which join together with remnants of the equatorial current to flow north and east, becoming the Gulf Stream. The Gulf Stream bathes the outer continental shelf of the United States and Canada, becoming the North Atlantic Drift, eastern limbs of which form to flow south again, becoming the Canary Current. Each of the great ocean basins have a similar set of boundary currents flowing around in vast gyres; in the Southern Hemisphere, the currents flow counterclockwise, a mirror of the Northern Hemisphere circulation patterns.

In prehistoric times, only wood and weeds drifted on the ocean surface. Coastal and shore vegetation torn away by storms went to sea: Trees, leaves, and great entangled mats of old wood and branches washed down the rivers, smaller seaweed tore away from shallow rocky pools, and giant kelps tore away from deeper bottom holdfasts. Detached algae were already colonized by mobile and attached species. Terrestrial vegetation that floated near shore was then colonized by coastal organisms—in some cases, the very sorts of species that would also encrust vessels such as the *Pelican*. Vegetation that went to sea carried these coastal colonizers with them but, in turn, were colonized by a suite of species that live only on drifting objects on the high seas: elegant, long-stalked pelagic barnacles (*Lepas*), neustonic crabs (*Planes*, *Portunus*, and *Pachygrapsus*), worms, sea slugs, and many other species. These species had evolved on natural floating substrates, reaching graceful pinnacles of diversity on the vast floating meadows of algae (*Sargassum*) in the Sargasso Sea in the middle of the North Atlantic Ocean.

And yet this natural floating world was also about to change as ships went to sea. Soon a vast new panoply of *objets de la mer* would begin to appear—the flotsam, jetsam, and detached lagan (goods lost or abandoned at sea) that were being generated by the thousands, and eventually millions, of pieces. And while the pelagic world had been a biodegradable one for eons, adding to the ocean mélange in the past century and more has been a sea of plastic; indeed, human activity has created a nearly *permanent* ocean of floating material. Vast islands of floating garbage have accumulated in the centers of small and large gyres. It has been argued that certain once-rare species are now common thanks to the availability of vastly more, and far more permanent, floating objects on which to attach on the ocean surface. At least for barnacles and pelagic crabs, at-sea real estate has never been better.

Ocean currents also transport plankton—permanent resident animals and plants whose three-dimensional world knows no hard surfaces. Zooplankton (the animal plankton of the sea, including copepods, jellyfish, and krill) and phytoplankton (the plant plankton of the sea, including diatoms and red-tide forming dinoflagellates) move *with* the currents; larger organisms, the nekton (such as fish, mammals, turtles, and squid), can move *against* ocean currents. Also in the plankton are the dispersal propagules—the gametes and larvae—of species that otherwise live on the seabed, or on rocks, pilings, piers, or ship bottoms. Depending upon the species, some larvae live only for a few hours in the water column; others may drift for weeks or months.

And so it is that the Gulf Stream entrains barnacle-covered sea buoys and snail larvae in the Western Atlantic and carries them east to Europe. Drift bottles released a few miles off the south side of Cape Cod will, months later, wash ashore in the Azores, while others will then reach Morocco before turning west to the Caribbean and the beaches of Georgia. Other bottles from America will wash ashore in the Bay of Biscay or Scotland.

What, then, made the voyage of the *Pelican* such a momentous event in the history of our planet's biota?

Ocean currents tend to move organisms within ocean basins; they do not mix the seas, except for the southern seas around the Cape of Good Hope and Cape Horn, for example. In addition, coastal currents, those in inshore waters flowing along the continental shelves, may mix only occasionally on their edges with the great ocean currents further offshore. Coastal waters are often characterized by salinities, temperatures, and productivity that, combined, create unique habitats for shallow-water (neritic) organisms.

In contrast, ocean currents, and the high seas themselves, are a completely different habitat, with different salinity, temperature, oxygen, and nutrient signatures, and often with far less productivity (and thus less food). The results in terms of biodiversity are not surprising: If we sample plankton in the inshore waters near Boston or Plymouth harbor, and then sample the plankton a few hundred miles offshore of these ports, there may be *no* species in common. Thus, the organisms of the coastline do not commonly hitchhike on ocean currents. When we sample drifting wood and plastic on the high seas, some of which has clearly come from a shore source, the wood is richly covered with mid-ocean animals and plants but rarely with colonists from the coastal zone, which apparently succumb to the harsh physical and chemical conditions of the open ocean.

Rare events occur, and such rare episodes over millennia may lead to distant colonization by natural (nonhuman-mediated) means. As the Hawaiian Islands appeared above the sea surface tens of millions of years ago, they were slowly colonized by terrestrial and marine life that drifted in from around the Pacific Rim. Many of these organisms came from the Indo-Pacific Ocean, a vast expanse of water, islands, and continental margins. Some of these organisms came from the Eastern Pacific Ocean, traveling by ocean currents from the warmer waters of Panamic shores or from the cooler climate of western North America. Drift bottles—or redwood trees—released off southern Oregon will, in some months, wash ashore in the Hawaiian archipelago. Shore snails and shore barnacles appeared on the Hawaiian Islands naturally, and thus represented those rare propagules that did not die on a high-seas journey. Given enough time, given tens and hundreds of thousands and millions of years, some organisms survive journeys across the seas.

But—and this is the difference that seafaring humans make—crossing the sea on ocean currents (even if takes millions of years via sweepstakes dispersal) or moving down continental margins on coastal currents is, at day's end, *predictable*. Natural global bioflow occurs along corridors: the edges of continents, along island chains, along ocean currents, and so on. By contrast, human-mediated global bioflow is *unpredictable*. Neither birds nor beetles, neither sea anemones nor seaweeds, naturally move between Rio de Janeiro and Hong Kong, or between Sydney and Seattle. Today, we can move almost any species anywhere in the world, advertently or inadvertently, within twenty-four hours. There is no precedent for the scale of this dispersal in time and space in the history of the Earth. Global homogenization is now in play.

Adding Complexity—and Species— to the Vector World

By the mid-1800s, thousands of wooden ships laden with thousands of species were sailing the globe. Few shores, whether continents or islands, remained unvisited. Cultural, economic, and military events punctuated the traditional paths of exploration, colonization, and port growth and development.

One such event was the California Gold Rush. From the late 1840s to the mid-1850s, tens of thousands of people poured into the Pacific coast of North America to seek gold, to sell merchandise to the gold seekers, or to establish the businesses and trades and support services for burgeoning cities such as San Francisco, whose populations grew from hundreds of people to tens of thousands within a few years. Ships arrived from the world over: New England, Europe, South America, Australasia, and Asia.

From a marine-biological point of view, this was one of the most rapid, focused, and massive movements of marine life in history. The port of San Francisco became a forest of the masts of ships abandoned for the gold fields. For a barnacle born in Boston, the scenario could hardly be better: For those hull-dwelling organisms that had survived two voyages through tropical waters from New England around the Horn to the Golden Gate, opportunity was now in hand for long-term residency in San Francisco Bay, acclimation to a new environmental regime, feeding, and reproduction. The ubiquitous New England acorn barnacle (*Balanus improvisus*) thus appeared on Bay wharves by 1853—and remains one of the most abundant barnacles there today.

COMMERCIAL OYSTERS: TRANSPLANTING ENTIRE COMMUNITIES ACROSS THE WORLD

New Englanders now began to dominate once Spanish-ruled cities, and cultural shifts commenced. Human colonists brought familiar foods with them, and ships loaded with such foods started arriving regularly in San Francisco, but one of the most favored eastern foods, the Atlantic oyster (*Crassostrea virginica*), rarely survived the 90- to 120-day ship voyages from the Atlantic to the Pacific. Although clipper ships were racing to the Pacific in the 1850s and 1860s, they could not move fast enough for human needs. Begun in 1863, the Transcontinental Railroad was designed to link east with west. The last spike driven in Promontory, Utah, on May 10, 1869, completing the railroad, had an unintended prophecy written on one side: "May God continue the unity of our Country as this Railroad unites the two great Oceans of the world."

Now eastern goods began to flow across the continent by rail, and by late 1869 and early 1870, railroad cars full of oysters, to be planted out in San Francisco Bay, began to arrive. In the next few decades, hundreds of carloads of eastern oysters were laid out in nearly every bay, estuary, and harbor from British Columbia to Southern California, as oystermen dreamed of establishing permanent harvestable populations on the West Coast. While the Atlantic oyster never successfully reproduced in large numbers, many other species did, since in the early days of transporting commercial oysters across the country, little or no effort was made to remove the many animals and plants—including the predators!—that characterize oyster beds. Soon species from Long Island Sound that were attached to the oysters, or were in the mud and seaweed stuffed into the oyster barrels, began to flourish in San Francisco Bay and other estuaries along the Pacific coast. Ironically, many of these came to dominate West Coast bays, even as the oysters, and the Atlantic oyster industry, began to die out due in part to the expanding human populations; hence the increased sewage and water-quality deterioration of the very estuaries where oysters could be grown.

By the 1890s, after legions of ships and millions of oysters had arrived from the Eastern Seaboard, the best guide to the marine life of San Francisco Bay was a guidebook to the marine life of New England. This biological revolution heralded the events of the coming century. Over the next hundred years, edible oysters—with as many as fifty species of epibionts (surface dwellers) on one oyster shell, and sometimes oyster predators, parasites, and pathogens—were moved around the world. As the Atlantic oyster industry faded away in the 1920s on the American Pacific coast, a new industry began to import shiploads rather than carloads of Japanese oysters (*Crassostrea gigas*) to western North America. The Japanese oyster would eventually reproduce and form natural beds in the Pacific Northwest (where it remains common today and the basis for an important commercial industry), and as a result, over the next fifty years, a substantial cross-section of

Japanese estuarine and salt-water species was introduced to the Northeastern Pacific Ocean. Japanese and Atlantic estuarine life had converged on American Pacific shores.

BALLAST ROCKS TO BALLAST WATER

Continental-scale railroads ("iron horses") began to flourish during the same era that wooden sailing ships were giving way to iron steam ships. With iron ships came bulkheaded holds, and steam engines meant that seawater could be pumped aboard ships for ballast, replacing a millennia worth of able-bodied seamen loading and unloading ballast rocks by hand. By the 1880s, ballast water tanks had become standard in ship design. Water ballast now began to move a new array of species that had not previously been in motion on ship bottoms, or amongst ballast rocks, or on oysters. Whatever was adjacent to the ship was brought into the ship— plankton, fish, seaweed, and floating debris with fouling and benthic (bottom-dwelling) species. Neritic, free-swimming organisms previously coastal-bound now sailed through ocean barriers, protected in the holds of ships—through ocean currents and across the mid-ocean, or through the freshwater locks of the Panama Canal. By the 1980s and 1990s, seawater ballast had become the major interoceanic vector for marine life, with an estimated five thousand and more species moving in ballast around the world every twenty-four hours (though the next day, of course, they would not be the same five thousand species).

CANALS, AIRPLANES, SEA FOOD,
AQUARIUMS, BAIT, THE BIOWEB, AND MORE

It would be pleasant to report that the combination of ships with vast growths of marine life on their hulls and life-laden ballast (be it rock or water), on the one hand, and the globalization of heavily fouled oysters, on the other, completes the story of the interface between marine biology and maritime history and of the stages that were set for the invasions of thousands of species around the world. But this is only the beginning of the story.

In 1800, the European shore crab *Carcinus maenas* had only two means to go to sea and see the world: amongst ballast rocks or in shipworm galleries on wooden vessels. British ships brought *Carcinus* to New England, where it became well-established and where—as we can now reconstruct two hundred years later (there were no marine biologists in America when the shore crab first arrived)—it had a profound impact on the ecology and biology of American Atlantic shores, as discussed below.

By 1900, opportunities for *Carcinus's* global voyaging had doubled. Two vectors were now in play that had not existed a century before: the movement of commercial oysters, and ballast water. Perhaps safe in a water ballast hold, *Carcinus* then appeared by the 1890s in Australia.

By 2000, the global vectors of 1900 had doubled again, with at least eight mechanisms available that could disperse *Carcinus* around the world: three vectors of earlier centuries (ballast rocks were now gone), along with a bait-worm industry (marine worms packed in seaweed shipped from Maine around the world); semi-submersible self-propelled exploratory petroleum platforms (sitting on continental shelves, rather than in ports and harbors); the movement of many additional live seafood products, thanks to the advent of airplanes (mussels, clams, and lobsters, with *Carcinus* amongst them); the marine aquarium pet trade industry; and marine biological supply houses. And thus it was that *Carcinus* appeared in South Africa in 1983 (perhaps via petroleum rigs), in 1989 in San Francisco Bay (thanks to the bait-worm/algal dunnage industry), and in 1984 and 2000 in Japan and Argentina (by means of ballast water, whose global volume had grown logarithmically by the end of the twentieth century).

Nor were these many new vectors all there was to the story. In the 1800s and 1900s, interoceanic and intracoastal canals were shortening sea routes and providing new corridors to connect long-isolated oceans, basins, and sounds. The sea-level Suez Canal, opened in 1869, linked the Mediterranean to the much greater diversity of the Red Sea and the Indian Ocean. Hundreds of species began to pour into, and spread out, through the Mediterranean Sea—a process that came to be known as lessepsian migration, named after the canal's builder, Ferdinand de Lesseps.

The Panama Canal, a lock canal opened in 1914, seemed to create a natural barrier by virtue of a huge mid-canal freshwater lake that would prevent marine life from flowing between the Atlantic and Pacific oceans. But early observations in England revealed living ship-hull barnacles that, able to hold their physiological (osmoregulatory) breath, had made it through the canal alive. But more important was ballast water—tiny seas of plankton carried by ships through the freshwater barrier, from east to west and west to east. While ships had been carrying ballast water around Cape Horn for decades, the Panama Canal vastly reduced transit time between oceans—and thus increased the survival of ballast water life by significantly reducing the length of the voyage. Other canals in Europe and America (especially the Cape Cod Canal, opened in Massachusetts in 1914) broke through classic barriers that had come to mark provincial or regional biodiversity boundaries.

With the public commercialization of the Internet and the World Wide Web, and the concomitant support of twenty-four-hour global delivery systems, a staggering number of live animals and plants are now available for open, unregulated purchase and transport. This "bioweb" is rich with unintended epibiota, as the organisms being shipped are often accompanied by a suite of additional species in the packing materials or on the animals and plants themselves—an interesting twenty-first-century repetition of the nineteenth-century transcontinental and transoceanic movements of "dirty" shellfish. A large number of exotic organisms are thereby placed in the hands of the public, a form of biological roulette whose consequences are impossible to define precisely.

THE INVADED OCEANS

Centuries of consistent movement of marine life—by a plethora of vectors—have resulted in a profound alteration of the biodiversity and ecological structure of many of the world's shorelines, and, in some cases, offshore open ocean waters as well. Some examples follow.

The Long-Invaded Mediterranean
Now Goes Tropical

In the central and western Mediterranean, immense, luxurious meadows of the Australian green seaweed *Caulerpa taxifolia* now carpet many square miles of the sea floor. Released accidentally from the Monaco Aquarium in the 1980s, and spread by currents and boats, *Caulerpa* has formed monocultural stands where formerly diverse native communities of seagrass, corals, bryozoans, and many other species once flourished. (Now banned in a number of countries, *Caulerpa* also established a population, released from a home aquarium tank, in a lagoon near San Diego in the 1990s, requiring a five-year, $7 million dollar eradication program.) The Mediterranean Sea has sustained more than five hundred exotic species invasions since the early 1900s; how many species invaded prior in early centuries is not known. At the beginning of the twenty-first century, the Mediterranean is undergoing a process known as *tropicalization*: As the Mediterranean continues to warm, southern species are establishing and becoming common, and warm-affinity species already present are becoming more abundant.

American and Asian Species
Become European "Natives"

In Western Europe, some of the most abundant species hail from distant shores. Early invasions began with Vikings returning from North America: By the 1100s, the American softshell clam *Mya arenaria* was appearing in Norse middens in Northern Europe. By the 1500s, new waves of invasions commenced with European ships returning from the Pacific. Portuguese sailors returned to Europe with the large Japanese oyster (*Crassostrea angulata*), a species that was first described in Europe in the 1700s and became culturally embedded as an iconic "native" species in the centuries to come. By the mid-1900s, marine biologists realized that the "Portuguese oyster" was in fact an Asian species (it was absent from the European fossil record and from pre-1500 shell middens), but fifty more years, and evidence gleaned from molecular biology, were needed to convince those who held the oyster as a cherished natural icon.

Importation of commercial oysters from America in the 1890s brought the slipper limpet (*Crepidula fornicata*) to England, where generations of children came to know it as the "native" boat shell on Brighton beaches. World War II brought the New Zealand barnacle *Austrominius modestus* to England, now one of the commonest seashore species along British and continental coasts. And it is said that on June 6, 1944, the hundreds of landing craft from the United Kingdom brought the slipper limpet to Normandy and continental Europe. In the 1970s, France imported air-cargo loads of the Japanese oyster *Crassostrea gigas* to outplant along Atlantic and Mediterranean shores. Many animals and plants came along with these oysters, prominent among them the Japanese seaweed *Sargassum muticum*, which invaded British shores and developed into massive beds that fouled boats and marinas. As the Japanese oyster culture on Atlantic French shores then grew, the Atlantic slipper limpet flourished and became a major nuisance species for the shellfish industry. Hundreds of alien species, from all over the world, are now common from Scandinavia to Gibraltar.

The Shores of Eastern Canada and New England Are Reshaped

Beginning in colonial times, North America's Atlantic shores were invaded by European and other species transported on and in ships. Our picture of colonial-era invasions (as with early invasions in Europe) remains clouded, however, as hundreds of years of post-invasion dispersal can mimic "natural" geographic patterns. "Baseline" surveys from the 1800s permit clearer detection of invasions of the past two centuries.

One of the best-documented invasions, anywhere in the ocean, was the arrival of the "English periwinkle" (*Littorina littorea*) in Canada and the Unites States at the beginning of the nineteenth century. Famous in England as an edible snail (tens of thousands of pounds turned up annually in London markets in the 1800s), it came ashore either in rock ballast or, in the 1830s, as an intentional planting in the Gulf of St. Lawrence. By the 1850s, it had reached Halifax on the outer coast of Nova Scotia (or was separately introduced again), and from there it took but thirty years to sweep down the coast to Cape May, New Jersey.

Reconstruction of the structure of pre-littorine America suggests that profound alterations of the flora and fauna of rocky shores, mudflats, marshes, and other habitats occurred in a matter of a few decades. Green algae gave way to beds of inedible brown seaweeds, some native snails declined, and hermit crabs flourished in a new shell resource—but in fact we have only a coarse picture of what New England may have looked like prior to the pressures exerted by billions of herbivorous, and occasionally carnivorous, one-inch-tall (2.5-centimeter) snails. The European omnivorous shore crab *Carcinus maenas*—a consumer of shellfish, barnacles, worms, seaweeds, and almost anything else it could grasp and tear apart—had arrived around 1800 in Long Island Sound, south of Cape Cod, and began to head north in the 1890s. By the beginning of the twentieth century, Boston shores were becoming dominated by two abundant European consumers.

It would have been difficult to imagine any species displacing or replacing *Carcinus*—a species of not only catholic trophic breadth but great physiological plasticity as well. Yet in 1988, a biology class from Franklin & Marshall College on a field trip to Cape May, New Jersey, collected the first specimens of a small crab, the Japanese shore crab *Hemigrapsus sanguineus*, in the Atlantic Ocean. Released by ballast water from inbound cargo ships, *Hemigrapsus* soon began spreading and, by 1993, had reached southern New England. By 2003, it had become the most common shore crab from New York to Cape Cod, and all other shore crabs, including the once-prevalent *Carcinus*, had become uncommon (and in some cases completely absent) on rocky shores. *Carcinus* persisted subtidally, apparently below the depth at which *Hemigrapsus* can flourish. The Japanese shore crab now occurs from Chesapeake Bay to Maine, and may continue north into Canada, especially with warming waters.

Floats, buoys, pilings, and boat bottoms are now often dominated by a host of exotic seasquirts (ascidians) and seaweeds from Europe and Asia. Non-native seasquirts form massive colonies from Florida to the Gulf of St. Lawrence. Particularly compelling is the 1990s colonization of offshore waters by one of these species, the Japanese colonial tunicate *Didemnum vexillum*, remarkable as the first-known invader of America's iconic fishing bank, Georges Bank. Although not predicted to make its way out to the open ocean, this weedy colonizer has, in retrospect, invaded one of the most disturbed ocean environments.

Over a hundred common non-native species now coat American Atlantic shores, while many more introduced species are uncommon, and many, many more are *cryptogenic*—a term referring to species that cannot be clearly identified as native or introduced. Five hundred years of ship traffic between North America and Europe have obscured the pre-shipping distribution of hundreds of species, whose historical biogeography can be reconstructed only painstakingly, species by species.

Hitchhikers Take Over San Francisco Bay

This bay in central California supports over three hundred exotic species—more than three times the number of invasions known for all of eastern Canada and New England. A combination of factors may be responsible for this high number. San Francisco Bay has been subject, since the 1850s, to many of the vectors outlined earlier in this chapter. While many ports and estuaries have been under the same invasion pressures, the hydrography and geology of the Bay are such that a great many species were able to colonize without being swept out to sea, a phenomenon known as the *lagoonal hypothesis* of invasions—in this case, on a vast scale.

In addition, San Francisco Bay appears to have had relatively few native species, as is also true of many other young Pacific-coast estuaries that were formed less than ten thousand years ago as the glaciers melted and the seas rose over a very narrow coastal shelf and flooded river-carved valleys (in contrast, for example, to American Atlantic estuaries, which formed on ancient broad continental shelves). While a low-diversity aboriginal bay fits the so-called *biotic resistance hypothesis* (in this case, helping to explain the ecosystem's low resistance to invasions), complicating the real-life scenario is that San Francisco Bay quickly came under the scourge of anthropogenic decimation, which turned it into the equivalent of an urban weedy lot. Hydraulic mining in the 1860s sent a river of sediment into the Bay, creating intertidal mud flats where the water had been sounded in the 1850s at twenty feet (six meters) and deeper. (Coincidental, and not human-caused, was the Great Flood of 1862, which turned parts of the Bay into a virtually freshwater ecosystem—no doubt eliminating, at least in shallow waters, large amounts of native biota.) Growing cities nearby poured untreated sewage into the Bay, resulting in serious pollution episodes. All of these processes may have laid the foundation for a highly invadable ecosystem.

Only a separate chapter would do justice to the breadth and depth of invasions in San Francisco Bay and other estuaries and bays on the Pacific coast of North America. In some of these bays and estuaries, 90 percent of the biomass comprises non-native species. Seawall communities in parts of San Francisco Bay are an intertwined amalgamation of Japanese, Australian, New England, and European species. A New Zealand warm-water rock-boring pillbug (*Sphaeroma quoianum*, an isopod crustacean), which arrived in the hulls of wooden ships in the late 1800s, has been swiss-cheesing bay shores from Southern California to San Francisco Bay for a century. Long restricted to California by the formerly cool waters of the Pacific Northwest, in the 1990s *Sphaeroma* arrived in Oregon's largest bay, Coos Bay, whose margins then began to rapidly deteriorate as millions of boring isopods flourished. The Chinese estuarine clam *Corbula amurensis*, a ballast water introduction of the 1980s, maintains densities of thousands per square meter on the floor of San Francisco, drawing off much of the water-column productivity.

Upon many other world shores, similar ecological conversions have played out:

- As recently as 1979, South Africa's rocky shores, first touched by European ships in the 1400s, have acquired the Mediterranean mussel *Mytilus galloprovincialis*, which now forms massive beds on open wave-swept coasts, displacing the native mussel *Aulacomya*.

- The most abundant high intertidal barnacle of Argentina is the California *Balanus glandula*, a 1970s arrival. Washing ashore on the sandy beaches below the same rocks is the Japanese kelp *Undaria pinnatifida*, a 1990s arrival.

- Over three hundred marine and estuarine invasions have colonized the Hawaiian Islands, a stopover and destination for sailing vessels since Captain James Cook's first visit in 1778. Today Pearl Harbor is a central repository of species from the Indo-Pacific, North America, Panama, the Caribbean, and Japan—a marine accidental zoo and accidental botanical garden. Arriving in the 1990s, the Caribbean barnacle *Chthamalus proteus* now forms an upper white band around Oahu's shores.

- In southern Australia, millions of Japanese seastars (*Asterias amurensis*) dominate Tasmania's Derwent estuary. Just to the north, waving beds of the Mediterranean tubeworm *Sabella spallanzanii* occupy the bottom of Port Phillip Bay.

And so the story goes, on and on, around the world. The American comb jelly *Mnemiopsis* invaded the Black Seas in the 1980s, decimating fisheries. Another comb jelly–eating comb jelly from the

Mediterranean, *Beroe*, then moved in, in the 1990s, moderating the *Mnemiopsis* population; but *Mnemiopsis* has now moved on, into the Caspian Sea. The Australian seasquirt *Pyura praeputialis* forms dense intertidal aggregations on the shores of Chile and outcompetes the native mussel *Peromytilus*, and the poisonous Pacific lionfish *Pterois volitans* is a common, aggressive carnivore along the Florida Keys, in the Caribbean, and up to the Carolina coast.

New invasions occur daily, and perhaps hourly, on ocean shores around the world. Our ability to recognize these, and to react, is modified, however, by the decreasing number of naturalists who explore such shores and, especially, by the decreasing number of taxonomists who can identify animals and plants. As a result, a great many invasions go unrecorded, although they may be by no means rare, or unimportant.

Managing Invasions and the Future of Marine Biodiversity

Several prominent aquatic invasions at the end of the twentieth century brought attention and management action to alien species introductions. The invasion of the Eurasian freshwater zebra and quagga mussels *Dreissena polymorpha* and *Dreissena bugensis* in North America in the 1980s (the spread of which cost hundreds of millions of dollars annually to control and manage), along with the invasion of toxic Japanese dinoflagellates in Australia (which impacted important seafood industries) at about the same time, precipitated global-scale interest in the management of ballast water. National-level (and at times regional-level) action plans were formulated, and the United Nations' International Maritime Organization (IMO) took ballast water under consideration throughout the 1990s.

Ballast water management strategy entails a ship's deballasting of coastal water in mid-ocean, reballasting, and then deballasting of high-seas water into the arrival port or harbor, thus eliminating the transfer of organisms between coastlines. However, the need for ship stability, especially in rough weather, and the inability of many vessels to remove all ballast water or ballast sediments, means that ballast exchange is a stopgap measure. At the same time, numerous mechanical (filtration), physical (heating or centrifugation), and chemical technologies are under consideration and experimentation for removing living organisms from ballast water. Such technologies would be installed aboard ships, through either new-vessel design or retrofitting. International and national laws and regulations are seeking to achieve such control in the first decades of the twenty-first century.

The many other vectors for species mobility—aquaculture, the live-seafood industry, bait, the bioweb, ship fouling, and more—require cooperative action across international and national lines. Economic, political, and social considerations often make progress difficult, though not impossible. Prevention of invasions has long been held to be the most important strategy, followed by early detection of new invasions (the latter known as *early detection/rapid response*). On land and in lakes, new invasions can at times be quickly surrounded and eradicated, but invasions in the open ocean often present a toothpaste-out-of-the-tube situation that is far more challenging.

Current trends offer reasons for both concern and optimism. On the one hand, we live in an era of rapidly increasing and evolving global trade (which concomitantly moves more and more species) and global climate change (which facilitates the arrival and success of many new invaders). On the other hand, there are now more conservation biologists, invasion biologists, restoration ecologists, and marine environmental managers than ever before in human history. Embedding at the earliest education levels—"larval imprinting"—the goal of preventing invasions will be a critical strategy for the coming decades.

Wildlife Trade and Invasive Species

CHRIS R. SHEPHERD AND LORETTA ANN SHEPHERD

Chris R. Shepherd and Loretta Ann Shepherd are a husband-and-wife team based in Malaysia. The pair has traveled extensively in the region and abroad, watching, photographing, and writing about wildlife. Both have dedicated their lives to conservation and are involved in a wide range of projects and activities.

Originally from Canada, Chris has been working in Southeast Asia on wildlife trade–related issues for eighteen years. For the past twelve years, he has been with the Southeast Asia regional program of TRAF-FIC, the wildlife trade monitoring network that works to ensure that trade in wild plants and animals is not a threat to the conservation of nature. As senior program officer, Chris conducts research on a wide variety of species groups, looking at legal and illegal trade dynamics and assessing the impact trade may have on wild populations. He also carries out enforcement assistance work in the region, which includes investigations and working closely with enforcement agencies around the world. In addition, Chris is an active member of many IUCN-SSC Specialist Groups (Otters, Bears, Cats, and Tortoises and Freshwater Turtles).

Loretta is the program coordinator of the Malaysian Conservation Alliance for Tigers (MYCAT), a joint program of four nongovernmental organizations supported by the Malaysian government for joint implementation of the National Tiger Action Plan for Malaysia. Loretta's main responsibility within MYCAT is coordination of communications and joint tiger conservation projects from its Secretariat's office. A former journalist with one of Malaysia's leading dailies, Loretta continues to write on wildlife issues in journals, books, and magazines.

In "Wildlife Trade and Invasive Species," Shepherd and Shepherd reveal the serious toll that the thoughtless global trade in wild animals is taking on our planet's biodiversity—and the ways in which pet owners and other well-intentioned animal lovers may be inadvertently contributing to the havoc created by rogue species.

The global trade in wildlife is worth billions of dollars each year. Many specimens entering the international market are acquired and traded illegally in violation of national and international laws and conventions.[1] Illegal and unsustainable wildlife trade is a leading threat to the conservation of thousands of species.

The focus of this chapter is Asia, where wild animals both dead and alive are traded for a number of purposes. The drivers of the trade are many; they include supplying the insatiable demand for luxury goods, novelty and subsistence consumption, use as ingredients in traditional medicines, the pet trade, supplying zoos, and in some parts of the world, especially Asia, religious purposes and magical beliefs. In addition to the pressures it places on native species, wildlife trade results in the introduction of non-native, often invasive species and their associated pests and diseases.

This isn't just a theoretical danger. Illegal and unsustainable trade, coupled with threats of habitat loss or degradation and associated factors, have led to major declines and near-extinctions of some of the world's most iconic creatures, including the tiger (*Panthera tigris*) and the Javan rhinoceros (*Rhinoceros sondaicus*). Numerous lesser-known creatures, such as the mainland serow (*Capricornis sumatraensis*), the straw-headed bulbul (*Pycnonotus zeylanicus*), the Sumatran laughingthrush (*Garrulax bicolor*), and the Burmese star tortoise (*Geochelone platynota*), are also slipping, largely unnoticed, into the abyss. The list of species threatened by the wildlife trade is a long one—and it keeps getting longer.

Southeast Asia in particular is a hotspot for illegal wildlife trade, with large volumes of animals being exported, imported, and re-exported and organized-crime syndicates increasingly involved. Imports of animals that are not native to Southeast Asia often involve species under extreme threat, many of them fetching large profits. Specimens of the ploughshare tortoise (*Astrochelys yniphora*), one of the most threatened reptiles in the world, are frequently offered for sale in Southeast Asia—for example, in the pet markets of Bangkok, Thailand, and Jakarta, Indonesia, as well as via the Internet.

Huge profits, of course, are the primary motivation for wildlife trade. As highlighted in a report produced by TRAFFIC on behalf of the World Bank, "What's Driving the Wildlife Trade?"—for which we consulted more than eighty experts on the wildlife trade in Cambodia, Indonesia, Lao People's Democratic Republic (formerly known as Laos), and Vietnam—the rising affluence in consumer countries in Asia, rather than poverty, is a major driver of demand for wildlife products in the region.[2]

The profit margins in the illegal wildlife trade rival those of the illicit drug trade. Some individual species, or their parts and derivatives, fetch thousands of dollars each. The rarer the species becomes, the more expensive it is, and with its acquisition come status and prestige.[3] Uncommon or geographically isolated species (e.g., island endemics) are in high demand; two examples are the Roti Island snake-necked turtle (*Chelodina mccordi*), which is found only on the small Indonesian island of Roti, and the Javan hawk-eagle (*Spizaetus bartelsi*), a national icon in Indonesia that is native to the island of Java.[4] Rare color varieties or morphs of species, especially reptiles and birds, are also in high demand in the pet trade.[5]

The result has been a tragic downward spiral: The graver the danger of extinction threatening an animal, the stronger the economic pressures that make its demise even more likely.

Some of the illegal wildlife trade supplies only local demand, but vast quantities of these animals are bound for international markets. Many of the species bartered across borders around the globe are traded live, to supply the increasing demand for pets and collections as well as for the meat trade. (Shipping live animals for the meat trade ensures that they arrive fresh and saves on the cost of installing and concealing refrigeration units on boats or planes.)

Few people realize the gargantuan scale of this trade. Millions of animals, including parts and products, are traded annually. Surveys conducted in wildlife markets in Myanmar between 1991 and 2006 revealed a total of 1,320 wild cat parts, representing a minimum of 1,158 individual animals.[6] In 2008, several seizures carried out within months of one another resulted in Malaysian authorities' confiscation of 1,236 dead owls, 9,423 live clouded monitor lizards (*Varanus nebulosus*), and legs from 47 sun bears (*Helarctos malayanus*).[7] The live animal trade alone is enormous. Singapore, for example, one of the most significant trade hubs for live birds, reported to the World Conservation Monitoring Centre–Convention on International Trade in Endangered Species of Wild Fauna and Flora (WCMC-CITES) Trade Database the legal exportation and re-exportation of more than 110,000 CITES-listed birds between 2005 and 2007, none of which involved species native to Singapore.

Shipments of animals are often measured in tons. From the city of Medan, Indonesia, for instance, about twenty-five tons of live, wild-caught, freshwater turtles and tortoises were exported to China each week during 1999 and 2000.[8] This resulted in severe depletion of local populations, and today only a few tons are harvested each month, with volumes continuing to decline.

Over-exploitation's direct effects on the future of species are obvious, but there are other less obvious—though equally destructive—impacts as well. One is the threat caused by the release, intentional or unintentional, of wildlife into areas to which they are not native. This link between the wildlife trade and invasive species is a dangerous one: Introduced wild animals have caused untold damage by preying on local species, competing for habitat, and spreading foreign disease, bacteria, and parasites. Animals imported into Southeast Asia often escape or are deliberately released by members of the public for perceived humane reasons, often connected to religious beliefs. The intensions aren't bad, but the introduced species may become invasive, forming viable populations that out-compete native species for food, territory, and habitat.[9]

The release of large volumes of animals is more than likely to have a severe, sometimes devastating impact on local wildlife populations. Picture a shipment of two tons of live cobras being dumped in one place—and imagine that you are a native mouse. Or picture a shipment of five tons of pangolins (scaly anteaters) being unloaded in a single patch of forest—and imagine that you are a pangolin already living in that same small forest patch, with just enough to eat.

Very little research has been carried out in Southeast Asia on the impact of such releases on native species. Studies need to be conducted and informed policies need to be developed—and, most important, implemented. Releasing non-native species has been shown time and again to have devastating effects on local wildlife around the world—but we're doing far too little to prevent this problem from increasing in the years to come.

RELEASE FOR MERIT

This is a wildlife management problem that is unique to Asia and driven by a cultural practice specific to the region. Throughout many parts of Asia, animals are purchased specifically for release into the wild, especially by the regions' Buddhist populations.[10] Although this practice is widely accepted and is often seen as an act of kindness—hence its name, "release for merit"—it has serious conservation and animal welfare implications.

Here's one example. The birds known as munias (*Lonchura* of various species), also called manikins or rice birds, are captured by the thousands to be released for merit. Preliminary studies have shown that mortality rates may be as high as 50 percent during capture and the first twenty-four hours in captivity.[11] Large numbers of munias are captured in Indonesia, where very little merit-release is practiced, and sent to neighboring Malaysia and Singapore for sale and release. Though socially accepted, this behavior is ecologically harmful and needs to be officially banned as well as discouraged through public education and, where necessary, prosecution of offenders.

WILDLIFE "RESCUE"

In some cases, well-intentioned animal lovers "rescue" exotic species from the squalor of shabby pet shops and set them free. These animals often perish, not being equipped for life in their new environment. From the perspective of animal welfare, such actions do nothing to "save" the animals. Others who survive and thrive go on to cause problems when they establish themselves where they do not belong.

Some animals, farmed for food, are purchased by well-intentioned but misguided welfare activists and released. For example, the American bullfrog (*Rana catesbeiana*), which is native to the central and eastern United States and farmed in many parts of Southeast Asia for local restaurant demand, can be a menace to local species when it escapes.[12] And the Chinese softshell turtle (*Pelodiscus sinensis*), which is native to eastern China, Korea, Taiwan, extreme southeastern Russia, Japan, and northern Vietnam, is farmed in vast quantities for the consumption market because of its "tonic" properties. Economically speaking, this highly carnivorous and aggressive turtle is an especially attractive species for farming, as it grows and breeds rapidly in tropical climates. Both large and small commercial operations to farm Chinese softshell turtles exist in Thailand, Malaysia, and Indonesia as well as in China and Taiwan.[13]

These animals frequently escape into water systems and quickly make themselves at home, out-competing local softshells and taking their toll on the local prey base. Although they have invaded numerous waterways, lakes, and ponds in Southeast Asia, their impact has not been sufficiently studied and steps to remedy this impact are yet to be taken.

Well-wishers beware: You are not doing these animals any favor when you release them into non-native habitats.

THE RED-EARED SLIDER INVASION

Some far less threatened species are also commonly offered for sale, in much greater volumes and for much less money. One such species is the red-eared slider (*Trachemys scripta elegans*). This attractive little freshwater turtle is one of three subspecies of the pond slider family from North America. Bred in the millions and sold at a very low price, it is the most popular species in the pet turtle trade and has earned the nickname "dime turtle." These low-cost pets are often purchased by people on a whim, or by people hoping to please their children on their birthday. As hatchlings, they are cute, easy to care for, and relatively hardy, which means they can survive certain levels of abuse: Owners can forget to feed them once in a while, carry them around in their hands, and push them around the fish tank like little speed boats. For these reasons, people think of sliders as a "good" pet for kids. But they don't catch Frisbees, do tricks, or run to the door to meet you when you get home. So kids get bored with them, and the turtles get larger and less appealing and start to bite. As a result, these turtles are often dumped into local drains and waterways.

According to one study, approximately 26 million red-eared sliders were exported from the United States to international markets between 1988 and 1994.[14] And the World Chelonian Trust has reported that between 2003 and 2005, an astounding 15,181,688 red-eared Sliders were exported from the United States.[15] Given such staggering numbers, it's no surprise that many sliders have established themselves in wilderness that is not part of their original range.

Many of these turtle hatchlings end up in Southeast Asia. According to the website of the Society for the Prevention of Cruelty to Animals (www.spca.org.sg/redsliders.html), approximately forty thousand red-eared sliders are imported into Singapore each month. Extrapolation from these data suggests that almost a half-million sliders arrive every year in the small island republic, where this species has become the most common turtle observed in the wild. Other nations such as Australia, France, Germany, Guam, Israel, Japan, South Africa, South Korea, and Thailand also report invasive populations of sliders,[16] and feral populations of this species have been found in Southeast and Far East Asia, Europe, the Caribbean, New Zealand, Israel, Bahrain, the Mariana Islands, Guam, and South Africa.[17] No wonder the red-eared slider was named one of the 100 World's Worst Invasive Alien Species on the Global Invasive Species database.[18]

GIANT MENACES

The impacts of invasive species have been researched and documented in special detail in Australia as well as in small island nations where extinctions, or near-extinctions, of endemic species have taken place. This is also especially true of the Florida Everglades, where big snakes like the Burmese python (*Python molurus*) make media headlines and resources to research invasive species issues are more readily available than elsewhere in the world.

A U.S. Geological Survey report released in October 2009 highlighted five non-native snakes (Burmese pythons, northern and southern African pythons, boa constrictors, and yellow anacondas) that are of "high risk" to the ecosystems of the United States, especially Florida. This report could be a step toward a ban on importing constrictorlike snakes into America. Unfortunately, no such measures have yet been taken in Southeast Asia.

PANGOLINS—AN ILLUSTRATION
OF THE SCALE OF THE TRADE

Pangolins (*Manis* of various species)—or scaly anteaters, as noted earlier—are taken from the wild and exported to China from Southeast Asian countries, mostly Indonesia and Malaysia, often via Lao PDR, Thailand, and Vietnam. Shipments of pangolins seized by authorities are so huge that many observers wonder how there can be any left in the wild. In March 2008, for example, twenty-four tons of frozen pangolins from Indonesia were seized in Vietnam. Months later, in July 2008, another seizure in Indonesia tipped the scales at over fourteen tons. At an average weight of between three and seven kilograms per animal,[19] these two seizures alone represent between 5,430 and 12,670 illegally harvested and traded individuals.

The greatest threat to the conservation of pangolins is illegal hunting for trade, largely to supply demand in China for meat and scales, used for tonics and traditional medicines.[20] Surveys in China have found that pangolins (live or just their scales) are commonly available in markets.[21] Pangolin parts are also used in other East Asian pharmacopoeia, such as in South Korea.[22] Scales are particularly targeted in the Chinese and other traditional medicines, and are considered the most valuable part of the pangolin in trade. The impact of this massive demand is rapidly becoming evident. According to individuals involved in the pangolin trade, the wild populations are being decimated; pangolins are scarce in countries such as Lao PDR, Cambodia, and Vietnam—countries closer to the end-consumer markets in China.

LIVE CONFISCATIONS—NOW WHAT?

The tremendous problems we've described so far obviously demand a law-enforcement response. Unfortunately, that is much easier to say than to carry out effectively.

Law-enforcement agencies around the world are struggling with the wildlife trade crisis. Most are underresourced and lack capacity. While many wildlife authorities are ill-equipped to handle criminal issues, police and customs officials are rarely expert in wildlife issues, and this makes for a situation easily taken advantage of by wildlife criminals. Today, however, significant effort is being invested in correcting this imbalance, through targeted capacity building training in wildlife trade hotspot areas, among other programs.

These enforcement support actions are improving the abilities of the authorities to intercept smuggling. But they are still left with the problem of what to do with confiscated live specimens.

While disposal of dead animals, parts, and derivatives is relatively straightforward, dealing with live specimens is a completely different story, a situation that law-enforcement agencies struggle with daily. Malaysian authorities, for instance, have made at least thirty-four pangolin seizures and confiscated a total of six thousand specimens, most of them live animals, over the past seven years. There are few viable options available in cases where seizures of non-native species are made. Repatriation is expensive and generally possible only if the place of origin can be unequivocally determined and if the native country desires the return of the animals.

Also insufficient is the number of rescue facilities equipped to cope with large numbers of often weak and injured animals, or to hold them for indefinite periods of time. Extremely constrained resources mean that government agencies understandably give the highest priority to native species rehabilitation. Authorities often shy away from euthanasia, perceiving it as contrary to their beliefs or even, rather ironically, as inhumane. As a result, the release of these live specimens is often considered the best solution available, often with no regard to the animals' origins, making the invasive species problem even greater.

In many countries in Southeast Asia, it is the authorities who release the non-native species; indeed, it is common practice to recommend immediate release for confiscated pangolins in this region.[23] In Vietnam, this may be due to the very high mortality rate (approaching 100 percent) of pangolins transferred to captive centers in the past. There is also a common perception that release "into the wild" will be less stressful than transfer to captivity, even when the origins of the confiscated animals are unknown.[24] Immediate release of confiscated animals requires minimal resources, is relatively quick, and can provide a positive public perception.

But releasing confiscated pangolins of unknown origins to the wild is not, in fact, a humane solution. Without prior disease screening, suitable quarantine, and the rehabilitation of sick or debilitated specimens, the individual pangolins will generally fare poorly. What's more, ill-considered release programs have the potential to alter the genetic makeup of existing pangolin populations and pose a significant disease risk for wild species at the release site.[25]

CONCLUSION

Sad to say, wildlife crime is still viewed as a low priority throughout Southeast Asia, indicating that the expertise and resources to deal with it are seriously inadequate. Policies to deal with confiscated animals are generally absent. With each IUCN Red List of Threatened Species assessment, the list of species being pushed closer to extinction grows longer.[26]

We urgently need improved legislation and increased enforcement to control the release of invasive species. Unfortunately, the enforcement agencies charged with the protection and conservation of wildlife often contribute to the problem themselves. Even when it is well-meaning, the release of confiscated specimens in areas where they are not native creates a threat to native wildlife and endangers the released animals themselves. Large numbers of such animals will undoubtedly deplete food sources in the vicinity of release and will starve. Furthermore, many of the released specimens are weak, sick, and ridden with parasites; most probably die shortly after release. Those that survive and become established have an impact on the environment that is generally unknown, since post-release monitoring is lacking.

What is to be done? One study has recommended that national laws, strategies, and guidelines be established to prevent and control alien invasive species.[27] Public education about the dangers of releasing pets and releasing animals for merit is urgently needed. And the authorities themselves need to be made aware of the consequences of dumping confiscated wildlife so that law-enforcement efforts to deal with the problem don't become a further conservation threat.

Planet of Weeds

DAVID QUAMMEN

David Quammen's eleven books include fiction, essays, and the nonfiction titles *The Song of the Dodo*, *Monster of God*, and *The Reluctant Mr. Darwin*. He is also the general editor of an illustrated edition of Charles Darwin's *On the Origin of Species*. He has received an Academy Award from the American Academy of Arts and Letters, a Guggenheim fellowship, the John Burroughs Medal for nature writing, and (three times) the National Magazine Award, most recently for "Was Darwin Wrong?," a 2004 cover story in *National Geographic*. (The answer to that title's question was: Not where it mattered most.)

Quammen is a contributing writer for *National Geographic*, publishes also in *Harper's* and other magazines, and has recently finished a three-year term as Wallace Stegner Professor of Western American Studies at Montana State University. His essay "Planet of Weeds" appeared first in *Harper's* (1998) and has since been reprinted in *Best American Essays 1999* (edited by Edward Hoagland), in *American Earth* (edited by Bill McKibben), and in an expanded edition (2008) of his own early collection, *Natural Acts*. His current book project involves the ecology and evolution of scary viruses. He lives in Montana with his wife, Betsy Gaines, a conservationist, and travels on assignment, by preference to jungles, deserts, and swamps.

EDITOR'S NOTE: *We asked David Quammen to provide us with a current update for his classic article on invasive species, "Planet of Weeds," and here is what he wrote:*

This piece was first published by *Harper's Magazine* in 1998. The circumstances of its conception were as follows. One day that spring Colin Harrison, then Deputy Editor of *Harper's*, called me and said: David, I want an essay on the subject of whether we're destroying the planet, and I think you're the person to write it. I asked Colin what he meant by the phrase, "destroying the planet," which to me sounded vague and wooly. He said: Tell me what *you* would mean. Um, okay. I described a general framework of ideas—the sixth mass extinction, the slow pace at which biological diversity recovers, the causes of extinction, including habitat loss, habitat fragmentation, and invasive species of the sort that ecologists call "weedy." I added two clear stipulations: (1) that Earth as a planet will of course continue circling on its orbit no matter what forms of malfeasance we humans commit, and (2) that the extinction of *Homo sapiens* is *not* a likely consequence of such malfeasance. Yes! said Colin, that's what I mean too! Write it! So I did.

Colin edited the essay, deftly but lightly, and it ran as the *Harper's* cover story that October, behind an apt cover image by the great postmodern biological artist Alexis Rockman. You could look it up.

People sometimes ask me whether, if I had that essay to write today, I would place concerns about climate change more prominently among my litany of dire anthropogenic factors. My answer to that question is not *Yes* and it's not *No*. My answer is: *Hello, aren't you thinking carefully about what's going on here?* My own view is that climate change is important (very important) mainly because it's a subcategory of the larger problem of mass extinctions, not the other way around. It's a subcategory of that problem because it exacerbates the effects of three factors depleting biological diversity: habitat loss, habitat fragmentation, and invasive species. I've been watching the climate-change issue unfold for thirty years and I've always felt that people were unclear in their minds as to why we should be so concerned. Catastrophic alterations in weather that cause inconvenience, misery, and death to humans, especially in low-lying coastal areas? Disruptions of agriculture? Loss of sovereign island nations? Spread of infectious human diseases to areas they hadn't previously reached? Yes, those will be lamentable events—but their consequences won't linger for tens and hundreds of millennia. Humans will adapt. They will move. They will innovate. They will make adjustments.

The one thing that can't be adjusted away is extinction of other species on a massive scale—extinction that vastly outpaces the rate at which new species can arise. Ten million years at minimum, Dave Jablonski estimates (see the piece), will be required for Earth to recover its full complement of species diversity after we've relinquished our dominance of Earth—if we ever do. And even 10 million years will not be enough to recreate the unique creatures that have been lost. Don't be distracted. Don't be gulled. When the polar bear, *Ursus maritimus*, disappears from this planet, it's gone from the universe forever. That's the bad news.

What follows is "Planet of Weeds," its message still relevant (alas) more than a decade later. This is my slightly revised version, prepared for inclusion in the expanded edition (2008) of my book *Natural Acts*. The sole differences between this version and what ran in *Harper's* is that I have restored here certain brief passages— e.g., the bit about H. G. Wells and his Morlocks and Eloi—that were originally cut for space to fit the magazine.

Hope is a duty from which paleontologists are exempt. Their job is to take the long view, the cold and stony view, of triumphs and catastrophes in the history of life. They study the fossil record, that erratic selection of petrified shells, carapaces, bones, teeth, tree trunks, leaves, pollen, and other biological relics, and from it they attempt to discern the lost secrets of time, the big patterns of stasis and change, the trends of innovation and adaptation and refinement and decline that have blown like sea winds among ancient creatures in ancient ecosystems. Although life is their subject, death and burial supply all their data. They're the coroners of biology. This gives to paleontologists a certain distance, a hyperopic perspective beyond the reach of anxiety over outcomes of the struggles they chronicle. If hope is the thing with feathers, as Emily Dickinson said, then it's good to remember that feathers don't generally fossilize well. In lieu of hope and despair, paleontologists have a highly developed sense of cyclicity. That's why I recently went to Chicago, with a handful of urgently grim questions, and called on a paleontologist named David Jablonski. I wanted answers unvarnished with obligatory hope.

Jablonski is a big-pattern man, a macroevolutionist, who works fastidiously from the particular to the very broad. He's an expert on the morphology and distribution of marine bivalves and gastropods—or clams and snails, as he calls them when speaking casually. He sifts through the record of these mollusk lineages, preserved in rock and later harvested into museum drawers, to extract ideas about the origin of novelty. His attention roams back through 600 million years of time. His special skill involves framing large, resonant questions that can be answered with small, lithified clamshells. For instance: By what combinations of causal factor and sheer chance have the great evolutionary innovations arisen? How quickly have those innovations taken hold? How long have they abided? He's also interested in extinction, the converse of abidance, the yang to evolution's yin. Why do some species survive for a long time, he wonders, whereas others die out much sooner? And why has the rate of extinction—low throughout most of Earth's history—spiked upward cataclysmically on just a few occasions? How do those cataclysmic episodes, known in the trade as mass extinctions, differ in kind as well as degree from the gradual process of species extinction during the millions of years between? Can what struck in the past strike again?

The concept of mass extinction implies a biological crisis that spanned large parts of the planet and, in a relatively short time, eradicated a sizable number of species from a variety of groups. There's no absolute threshold of magnitude, and dozens of different episodes in geologic history might qualify, but five big ones stand out: Ordovician, Devonian, Permian, Triassic, Cretaceous. The Ordovician extinction, 439 million years ago, entailed the disappearance of roughly 85 percent of marine animal species—and that was before there *were* any animals on land. The Devonian extinction, 367 million years ago, seems to have been almost as severe. About 245 million years ago came the Permian extinction, the worst ever, claiming 95 percent of all known animal species and therefore almost wiping out the animal kingdom altogether. The Triassic, 208 million years ago, was bad again, though not nearly so bad as the Permian. The most recent was the Cretaceous extinction (sometimes called the K-T event because it defines the boundary between two geologic periods, with K for Cretaceous, never mind why, and T for Tertiary), familiar even to schoolchildren because it ended the age of dinosaurs. Less familiarly, the K-T event also brought extinction of the marine reptiles and the ammonites, as well as major losses of species among fish, mammals, amphibians, sea urchins, and other groups, totaling 76 percent of all species. In between these five episodes occurred some lesser mass extinctions, and throughout the intervening lulls extinction continued, too— but at a much slower pace, known as the background rate, claiming only about one species in any major group every million years. At the background rate, extinction is infrequent enough to be counterbalanced by the evolution of new species. Each of the five major episodes, in contrast, represents a drastic net loss of species diversity, a deep trough of biological impoverishment from which Earth only slowly recovered. How slowly? How long is the time lag between a nadir of impoverishment and a recovery to ecological fullness? That's another of Jablonski's research interests. His rough estimates run to 5 or 10 million years. What drew me to this man's work, and then to his doorstep, were his special competence on mass extinctions and his willingness to discuss the notion that a sixth one is in progress now.

Some people will tell you that we as a species, *Homo sapiens*, all six billion of us in our collective impact, are destroying the world. Me, I won't tell you that, because "the world" is so vague, whereas what we are or aren't destroying is quite specific. Some people will tell you that we are rampaging suicidally toward a degree of global wreckage that will result in our own extinction. I won't tell you that either. Some people say that the environment will be the paramount political and social concern of the twenty-first century, but what they mean by "the environment" is anyone's guess. Polluted air? Polluted water? Acid rain? Toxic wastes left to burble beneath neighborhood houses and malls? A frayed skein of ozone over Antarctica? Global warming, driven by the greenhouse gases emitted from smokestacks and cars? None of these concerns is of itself the big one, paleontological in scope, though some (notably, climate change) are closely entangled with it. If the world's air is clean for humans to breathe but supports no birds or butterflies, if the world's waters are pure for humans to drink but contain no fish or crustaceans or diatoms, have we solved our environmental problems? Well, I suppose so, at least as environmentalism is commonly construed. That clumsy, confused, and presumptuous formulation "the environment" implies viewing air, water, soil, forests, rivers, swamps, deserts, and oceans as merely a milieu within which something important is set: human life, human history. But what's at issue in fact is not an environment; it's a living world.

Here instead is what I'd like to tell you: The consensus among conscientious biologists is that we're headed into another mass extinction, a vale of biological impoverishment commensurate with the big five. Many experts remain hopeful that we can brake that descent, but my own view is that we're likely to go all the way down. I visited David Jablonski to ask what we might see at the bottom.

On a hot summer morning, Jablonski is busy in his office on the second floor of the Hinds Geophysical Laboratory at the University of Chicago. It's a large open room furnished in tall bookshelves, tables piled with books, stacks of paper standing knee-high off the floor. The walls are mostly bare, aside from a chart of the geologic time scale, a clipped cartoon of dancing tyrannosaurs in red sneakers, and a poster from a Rodin exhibition, quietly appropriate to the overall theme of eloquent stone. Jablonski is a lean forty-five-year-old man with a dark full beard. Educated at Columbia and Yale, he came to Chicago in 1985 and has helped make its paleontology program perhaps the country's best. Although in not many hours he'll be leaving on a trip to Alaska, he has been cordial about agreeing to this chat. Stepping carefully, we move among the piled journals, reprints, and photocopies. Every pile represents a different research question, he tells me. "I juggle a lot of these things all at once because they feed into one another." That's exactly why I've come: for a little rigorous intellectual synergy.

Let's talk about mass extinctions, I say. When did someone first realize that the concept might apply to current events, not just to the Permian or the Cretaceous?

He begins sorting back through memory. In the early and middle 1980s, he recalls, there occurred a handful of symposiums and lecture series on the subject of extinction, for which the rosters included both paleontologists and what he whimsically calls "neontologists," meaning biologists who study creatures that are still alive. An event was held at the Field Museum here in Chicago, with support from the National Science Foundation, that attracted four hundred scientists. Another, at which Jablonski himself spoke, took place at the New England Aquarium, in Boston. "The chronology is a little hazy for me," he says. "But one that I found most impressive was the Elliott meeting, the one in Flagstaff." David K. Elliott, of the geology department at Northern Arizona University, had pulled that gathering together in August of 1983 and later edited the invited papers into a volume titled *Dynamics of Extinction*. The headliner among the neontologists was Paul Ehrlich, eminent as an ecologist, widely famed for his best-selling jeremiad *The Population Bomb*, and co-author of a 1981 book on human-caused extinctions. Ehrlich spoke mainly about birds, mammals, and butterflies, sketching the severity of the larger problem and offering suggestions about what could be done. For the paleontological perspective, it was Jablonski again and a few others, including John Sepkoski and David Raup, later to be his colleagues at the University of Chicago. Sepkoski and Raup, while sorting through a huge body of data on the life spans of fossil groups, had lately noticed a startlingly regular pattern of recurrence—at about 26-million-year intervals—in the timing of large and medium-sized mass extinctions. The Sepkoski-Raup paper at Flagstaff, building on their own earlier work as well as the hot new idea that an asteroid impact had killed off the dinosaurs, suggested a dramatic hypothesis for explaining those recurrent mass extinctions: that maybe an invisible twin star (an "undetected companion," they called it) orbits mutually around our sun, returning every 26 million years and bringing with it each time, by gravitational pull, a murderous rain of interplanetary debris that devastates ecosystems and wipes out many species. Sepkoski's brief presentation of the idea was provocative enough to draw attention not just in *Science* and *Science News* but also the *Los Angeles Times*. Some people labeled that invisible companion "Nemesis," after the Greek goddess of vengeance, and others casually called it the Death Star. Meanwhile, another of the presentations at Flagstaff was attracting no such fuss, but that's the one Jablonski remembers now.

It was a talk by Daniel Simberloff, an ecologist then at Florida State University, highly respected for his incisive mind but notoriously reluctant to draw sweeping conclusions from limited data. Simberloff's remarks carried the title, "Are We on the Verge of a Mass Extinction in Tropical Rain Forests?" His answer, painstakingly reached, was yes.

"That's a really important paper, and a scary one," Jablonski says.

He vividly recalls the Flagstaff situation. "It wasn't a media event. It was scientists talking to scientists, being very up-front about what the uncertainties were and what the problems were." The problems were forest destruction, forest fragmentation, the loss of species that follows from those factors, and the cascading additional extinctions that come when ecosystems unravel. The uncertainties were considerable too, since there is no positive evidence left behind, no corpus delicti, when a species of rare bird or unknown beetle disappears as a consequence of the incineration of its habitat. Proving a negative fact is always difficult, and extinction is inherently a negative fact: *Such-and-such no longer exists.* Some biologists had begun warning of an extinction crisis that would be epochal in scale, their concern based on inference from the destruction of habitats that harbor vast numbers of highly localized species—in particular, tropical forests—and a few of those biologists had vivified their warnings with numerical estimates.

Simberloff set himself to a skeptic's question: Is the situation really so dire? From his own cautious inferences and extrapolations, he reported that, "even with an increase in the rate of destruction, there is not likely to be a mass extinction by the end of the century comparable to those of the geological past." He meant the twentieth century, of course. But was he saying that the alarums were illusory? Simberloff's reputation was such that no one could doubt he would make any unfashionable, spoilsport pronouncement to which the data, or lack of it, led him. Instead he added that, in the next century, "if there are no major changes in the way forests are treated, things may get much worse." His calculation suggested that, if tropical forests in the Americas were reduced to what's presently set aside as parks and reserves, 66 percent of all the native plant species would disappear by the end of the twenty-first century, and 69 percent of all Amazon birds. Yes, it would be a catastrophe on the same scale as every mass extinction except the Permian, Simberloff concluded.

"For me," David Jablonski says now, "that was a turning point."

But it's not the *starting* point I asked about. By the time of the Flagstaff meeting, I remind him, the idea of convening biologists together with paleontologists for a discussion of mass extinction was almost obvious, as reflected by the fact that two such events occurred that year. When was the idea less obvious? When was it just a fresh, counterintuitive notion? Jablonski obliges me by pushing his memory a little harder—back, as it turns out, to his own work during graduate school.

In the 1960s and early 1970s, concern about human-caused extinctions was neither widespread nor ecologically astute. Some writers warned about "vanishing wildlife" and "endangered species," but generally the warnings were framed around individual species with popular appeal, such as the whooping crane, the tiger, the blue whale, the peregrine falcon. Back in 1958, the pioneering

British ecologist Charles Elton had published a farsighted book about biological dislocations, *The Ecology of Invasions by Animals and Plants*; Rachel Carson in 1962, with *Silent Spring*, had alerted people to the widespread, pernicious effects of pesticides such as DDT; and David Ehrenfeld's *Biological Conservation* appeared in 1970. But those three were untypical in their grasp of larger contexts. During the 1970s a new form of concern broke forth—call it wholesale concern—from the awareness that unnumbered millions of narrowly endemic (that is, unique and localized) species inhabit the tropical forests and that those forests were quickly being cut. The World Wildlife Fund and the Smithsonian Institution sponsored a symposium in 1974 on the subject of biological impoverishment; the chief scientist at WWF and the main organizer of that event was a young ecologist named Thomas E. Lovejoy, not long removed from his own doctoral work on Amazon birds. Another early voice belonged to Norman Myers, a Berkeley-trained biologist based in Nairobi. In 1976 Myers published a paper in *Science* recommending greater attention to the economic pressures that drive habitat destruction and the consequent loss of species; in passing, he also compared current extinctions with the rate during what he loosely called, "the 'great dying' of the dinosaurs." David Jablonski, then a graduate student struggling to do his dissertation and pay his bills, read Myers's paper and tucked a copy into his files. The comparison to the Cretaceous extinction, an event about which he was knowledgeable, didn't seem to him incongruous. Soon afterward, in early 1978, Jablonski was running out of cash and so "finagled the opportunity" to offer a seminar course, a special elective for undergraduates, through one of the Yale residential colleges. "I decided to teach it on extinction," he says.

Now suddenly energized by this recollection, Jablonski dodges among his paper-pile stalagmites to a cabinet and returns with a twenty-year-old file. He flips through it, mesmerized like an old athlete over a scrapbook from his improbable youth. The yellowing sheets tell us that his course ran in autumn 1978 as college seminar 130a, "Crises in the Evolution of Life." Eleven weeks of class were devoted to paleontological fundamentals such as deep time, uniformitarian change, the tempo and mode of evolution, Darwin and Lamarck, Cuvier and Lyell, and then to signal episodes such as the Permian extinction, the Devonian extinction, the K-T event. Week twelve would connect paleontology with neontology. On that Tuesday evening, according to a typed outline saved in the old file, students would consider the past and future impact of *Homo sapiens*, concerning notably: "The diminution of global biotic diversity, and how (or if) it should be maintained. Climatic effects of human activities. Are we on the brink of a mass extinction? The past as the key to the present." It was the first class that David Jablonski ever taught.

Norman Myers's early role in this matter was important from several angles. "He was the guy who really started the quantification of extinction," Jablonski recalls. "Norman was a pretty lonely guy for a long time, on that." In 1979 Myers published *The Sinking Ark*, which explained the extinction problem for a popular audience, and in 1980 he produced a report to the National Academy of Sciences, drily titled *Conversion of Tropical Moist Forests* but full of eloquent data tracing the worldwide destruction of rainforest ecosystems. In the former book, he offered some rough numbers and offhanded projections. Between the years 1600 and 1900, by his count, humanity had caused the extinction of about 75 known species, almost all of them mammals and birds. Between 1900 and 1979, humans had extinguished another 75 known species. Repeating what he had said in *Science*, Myers noted that this provisional tally—totaling 150 known species, all lost in less than four centuries—was itself well above the rate of known losses during the Cretaceous extinction. But more worrisome was the inferable rate of unrecorded extinctions, recent and now impending, among tropical plants and animals still unidentified by science. He guessed that 25,000 plant species presently stood jeopardized, and maybe hundreds of thousands of insects. "By the late 1980s we could be facing a situation where one species becomes extinct each hour. By the time human communities establish ecologically sound life-styles, the fallout of species could total several million." Rereading those sentences now, I'm struck by the reckless optimism of his assumption that human communities eventually *will* establish "ecologically sound life-styles." But back in 1981, when I first encountered Myers's book, his predictions seemed shocking and gloomy.

A year after *The Sinking Ark* appeared, Tom Lovejoy of WWF offered his own cautionary guesstimate in a section of the *Global 2000* report to outgoing President Jimmy Carter. Based on current projections of forest loss and a plausible relationship between forest area and endemism, Lovejoy suggested that 15 to 20 percent of all species—amounting to millions—might be lost by the end of the twentieth century. In the course of his discussion, Lovejoy also coined a new phrase, "biological diversity," which seems obvious in retrospect but hadn't yet been in use for denoting the aggregate of what was at stake. The portmanteau version, "biodiversity," would be buckled together a few years later. Among field biologists a sense of focused concern was taking hold.

These early tries at quantification proved consequential for two reasons. First, Myers and Lovejoy helped galvanize public concern over the seemingly abstract matter of how many species may be lost as humanity claims an ever larger share of Earth's landscape and resources. Second, the Myers and Lovejoy warnings became targets for a handful of critics, who used the inexactitude of those numbers to cast doubt on the reality of the whole problem. Most conspicuous among the naysayers was Julian Simon, an economist at the University of Maryland, who argued bullishly that human population growth and human resourcefulness would solve all problems worth solving, of which a decline in diversity of tropical insects wasn't one.

In a 1986 issue of *New Scientist*, Simon rebutted Norman Myers, based on his own construal of select data, to the effect that there was "no obvious recent downward trend in world forests—no obvious 'losses' at all, and certainly no 'near catastrophic' loss." He later co-authored an op-ed piece in the *New York Times* under the headline "Facts, Not Species, Are Periled." Again he went after Myers, asserting a "complete absence of evidence for the claim that the extinction of species is going up rapidly—or even going up at all." Simon's worst disservice to logic in that statement and others was the denial that *inferential* evidence of wholesale extinction counts for anything. Of inferential evidence there was an abundance—for example, from the Centinela Ridge in a cloud-forest zone of western Ecuador, where in 1978 the botanist Alwyn Gentry and a colleague found thirty-eight species of narrowly endemic plants, including several with mysterious black leaves. Before Gentry could get back, Centinela Ridge had been completely deforested, the native plants replaced by cacao and other crops. As for inferential evidence generally, we might do well to remember what it contributes to our conviction that approximately 105,000 Japanese civilians died in the atomic bombing of Hiroshima. The city's population fell abruptly on August 6, 1945, but there was no one-by-one identification of 105,000 bodies.

Nowadays a few younger writers have taken Simon's line, pooh-poohing the concern over extinction. As for Simon himself, who died in 1998, perhaps the truest sentence he left behind was, "We must also try to get more reliable information about the number

of species that might be lost with various changes in the forests."
No one could argue.

But it isn't easy to get such information. Field biologists tend to
avoid investing their precious research time in doomed tracts of
forest. Beyond that, our culture offers little institutional support
for the study of narrowly endemic species in order to register their
existence *before* their habitats are destroyed. Despite these obstacles, recent efforts to quantify rates of extinction have supplanted
the old warnings. These new estimates use satellite imaging and
improved on-the-ground data about deforestation, records of the
many human-caused extinctions on islands, and a branch of ecological theory called island biogeography, which connects documented island cases with the mainland problem of forest fragmentation. These efforts differ in particulars, reflecting how much
uncertainty is still involved, but their varied tones form a chorus of
consensus. I'll mention three of the most credible.

W. V. Reid, of the World Resources Institute, in 1992 gathered
numbers on the average annual deforestation in each of sixty-three
tropical countries during the 1980s, and from them he charted
three different scenarios (low, middle, high) of presumable forest
loss by the year 2040. He chose a standard mathematical model of
the relationship between decreasing habitat area and decreasing
species diversity, made conservative assumptions about the crucial constant, and ran his various deforestation estimates through
the model. Reid's calculations suggest that by the year 2040, between 17 and 35 percent of tropical forest species will be extinct
or doomed to extinction. Either at the high or the low end of this
range, it would amount to a bad loss, though not as bad as the K-T
event. Then again, 2040 won't mark the end of human pressures
on biological diversity or landscape.

Robert M. May, an ecologist at Oxford, co-authored a similar effort in 1995. May and his colleagues noted the five causal factors that account for most extinctions: habitat destruction, habitat fragmentation, overkill, invasive species, and secondary effects cascading through an ecosystem from other extinctions. Each of those five is more intricate than it sounds. For instance, habitat fragmentation dooms species by consigning them to small parcels of habitat left insularized in an ocean of human impact, and by then subjecting them to the same jeopardies (small population size, acted upon by environmental fluctuation, catastrophe, inbreeding, bad luck, and cascading effects) that make island species especially vulnerable to extinction. May's team concluded that most extant bird and mammal species can expect average life spans of between 200 and 400 years. That's equivalent to saying that about a third of 1 percent will go extinct each year until some unimaginable end point is reached. "Much of the diversity we inherited," May and his co-authors wrote, "will be gone before humanity sorts itself out."

The most recent estimate comes from Stuart L. Pimm and Thomas M. Brooks, ecologists at the University of Tennessee. Using a combination of published data on bird species lost from forest fragments and field data they gathered themselves, Pimm and Brooks concluded that 50 percent of the world's forest bird species will be doomed to extinction by deforestation occurring over the next half-century. And birds won't be the sole victims. "How many species will be lost if current trends continue?" the two scientists asked. "Somewhere between one third and two thirds of all species—easily making this event as large as the previous five mass extinctions the planet has experienced."

Jablonski, who started down this line of thought in 1978, offers me a reminder about the conceptual machinery behind such estimates. "All mathematical models," he says cheerily, "are wrong.

They are approximations. And the question is: Are they usefully wrong, or are they meaninglessly wrong?" Models projecting present and future species loss are useful, he suggests, if they help people realize that *Homo sapiens* is perturbing Earth's biosphere to a degree it hasn't often been perturbed before. In other words, that this is a drastic experiment in biological drawdown we're engaged in, not a continuation of routine.

Behind the projections of species loss lurk a number of critical but hard-to-plot variables, among which two are especially weighty: continuing landscape conversion and the growth curve of human population.

Landscape conversion can mean many things: draining wetlands to build roads and airports, turning tallgrass prairies under the plow, fencing savanna and overgrazing it with domestic stock, cutting second-growth forest in Vermont and consigning the land to ski resorts or vacation suburbs, slash-and-burn clearing of Madagascar's rainforest to grow rice on wet hillsides, industrial logging in Borneo to meet Japanese plywood demands. The ecologist John Terborgh and a colleague, Carel P. van Schaik, have described a four-stage process of landscape conversion that they call the land-use cascade. The successive stages are: (1) *wildlands*, encompassing native floral and faunal communities altered little or not at all by human impact; (2) *extensively used areas*, such as natural grasslands lightly grazed, savanna kept open for prey animals by infrequent human-set fires, or forests sparsely worked by slash-and-burn farmers at low density; (3) *intensively used areas*, meaning crop fields, plantations, village commons, travel corridors, urban and industrial zones; and finally (4) *degraded land*, formerly useful but now abused beyond value to anybody. Madagascar, again, would be a good place to see all four stages, especially the terminal one. Along a thin road that leads inland from a town called Mahajanga, on the west coast, you can gaze out over a vista of degraded land—chalky red hills and gullies, bare of forest, burned too often by graziers wanting a short-term burst of pasturage, sparsely covered in dry grass and scrubby fan palms, eroded starkly, draining red mud into the Betsiboka River, supporting almost no human presence. Another showcase of degraded land—attributable to fuelwood gathering, overgrazing, population density, and decades of apartheid—is the Ciskei homeland in South Africa. Or you might look at over-irrigated crop fields left ruinously salinized in the Central Valley of California.

Among all forms of landscape conversion, pushing tropical forest from the *wildlands* category to the *intensively used* category has the greatest impact on biological diversity. You can see it in western India, where a spectacular deciduous ecosystem known as the Gir forest (home to the last surviving population of the Asiatic lion, *Panthera leo persica*) is yielding along its ragged edges to new mango orchards, peanut fields, and lime quarries for cement. You can see it in the central Amazon, where big tracts of rainforest have been felled and burned, in a largely futile attempt (encouraged by misguided government incentives, now revoked) to pasture cattle on sun-hardened clay. According to the United Nations Food and Agriculture Organization, the rate of deforestation in tropical countries has increased (contrary to Julian Simon's claim) since the 1970s, when Norman Myers made his estimates. During the 1980s, as the FAO reported in 1993, that rate reached 15.4 million hectares (a hectare being the metric equivalent of 2.5 acres) annually. South America was losing 6.2 million hectares of forest a year. Southeast Asia was losing less in sheer area but more proportionally: 1.6 percent of its forests yearly. In terms of cumulative loss, as reported by other observers, the Atlantic coast forest of Brazil is at least 95 percent gone. The Philippines, once nearly covered with rainforest, has lost 92 percent. Costa Rica has continued to lose forest, despite that country's famous concern for its biological resources. The richest old-growth lowland forests in West Africa, India, the Greater Antilles, Madagascar, and elsewhere have been reduced to less than a tenth of their original areas. By the middle of the twenty-first century, if those trends continue, tropical forest will exist virtually nowhere outside of protected areas—that is, national parks, wildlife refuges, and other official reserves.

How many protected areas will there be? The present worldwide total is about 9,800, encompassing 6.3 percent of the planet's land area. Will those parks and reserves retain their full biological diversity? No. Species with large territorial needs will be unable to maintain viable population levels within small reserves, and as those species die away their absence will affect others. The disappearance of big predators, for instance, can release limits on medium-sized predators and scavengers, whose overabundance can drive still other species (such as ground-nesting birds) to extinction. This has already happened in some habitat fragments, such as Panama's Barro Colorado Island, and been well documented in the literature of island biogeography. The lesson of fragmented habitats is Yeatsian: Things fall apart.

Human population growth will make a bad situation worse by putting ever more pressure on all available land.

Population growth rates have declined in many countries within the past several decades, it's true. But world population is still increasing, and even if average fertility suddenly, magically dropped to 2.0 children per female, population would continue to increase (on the momentum of birth rate exceeding death rate among a generally younger and healthier populace) for some time.

The annual increase is now 80 million people, with most of that increment coming in less-developed countries. The latest long-range projections from the Population Division of the United Nations, released earlier this year, are slightly down from previous long-term projections in 1992 but still point toward a problematic future. According to the U.N.'s middle estimate (and most probable? that's hard to know) among seven fertility scenarios, human population will rise from the present 5.9 billion to 9.4 billion by the year 2050, then to 10.8 billion by 2150, before leveling off there at the end of the twenty-second century. If it happens that way, about 9.7 billion people will inhabit the countries included within Africa, Latin America, the Caribbean, and Asia. The total population of those countries—most of which are in the low latitudes, many of which are less developed, and which together encompass a large portion of Earth's remaining tropical forest—will be more than twice what it is today. Those 9.7 billion people, crowded together in hot places, forming the ocean within which tropical nature reserves are insularized, will constitute 90 percent of humanity. Anyone interested in the future of biological diversity needs to think about the pressures these people will face, and the pressures they will exert in return.

We also need to remember that the impact of *Homo sapiens* on the biosphere can't be measured simply in population figures. As the population expert Paul Harrison pointed out in his book *The Third Revolution*, that impact is a product of three variables: population size, consumption level, and technology. Although population growth is highest in less-developed countries, consumption levels are generally far higher in the developed world (for instance, the average American consumes about ten times as much energy as the average Chilean, and about a hundred times as much as the average Angolan), and also higher among the affluent minority in any country than among the rural poor. High consumption exacerbates the impact of a given population, whereas technological developments may either exacerbate it further (think of the automobile, the air conditioner, the chainsaw) or mitigate it (as when a technological innovation improves efficiency for an established function). All three variables play a role in every case, but a directional change in one form of human impact—upon air pollution from fossil-fuel burning, say, or fish harvest from the seas—can be mainly attributable to a change in one variable, with only minor influence from the other two. Sulfur-dioxide emissions from developed countries fell dramatically during the 1970s and '80s, due to technological improvements in papermaking and other industrial processes; those emissions would have fallen still farther if not for increased population (accounting for 25 percent of the upward vector) and increased consumption (accounting for 75 percent). Deforestation, in contrast, is a directional change that *has* been mostly attributable to population growth.

According to Harrison's calculations, population growth accounted for 79 percent of the deforestation in less-developed countries between 1973 and 1988. Some experts would argue with those calculations, no doubt, and insist on redirecting our concern toward the role that distant consumers, wood-products buyers among slow-growing but affluent populations of the developed nations, play in driving the destruction of Borneo's dipterocarp forests or the hardwoods of West Africa. Still, Harrison's figures point toward an undeniable reality: More total people will need more total land. By his estimate, the minimum land necessary for food growing and other human needs (such as water supply and waste dumping) amounts to one-fifth of a hectare per person. Given the U.N.'s projected increase of 4.9 billion souls before the human population finally levels off, that comes to another billion hectares of human-claimed landscape, a billion hectares less forest—even without allowing for any further deforestation by the current human population, or for any further loss of agricultural land to degradation. A billion hectares—in other words, 10 million square kilometers—is, by a conservative estimate, well more than half the remaining forest area in Africa, Latin America, and Asia. This raises the vision of a very exigent human population pressing snugly around whatever patches of natural landscape remain.

Add to that vision the extra, incendiary aggravation of poverty. According to a recent World Bank estimate, about 30 percent of the total population of less-developed countries lives in poverty. Alan Durning, in his 1992 book *How Much Is Enough? The Consumer Society and the Fate of the Earth*, puts it in a broader perspective when he says that the world's human population is divided among three "ecological classes": the consumers, the middle-income, and the poor. His consumer class includes those 1.1 billion fortunate people whose annual income per family member is more than $7,500. At the other extreme, the world's poor also number about 1.1 billion people—all from households with less than $700 annually per family member. "They are mostly rural Africans, Indians, and other South Asians," Durning writes. "They eat almost exclusively grains, root crops, beans, and other legumes, and they drink mostly unclean water. They live in huts and shanties, they travel by foot, and most of their possessions are constructed of stone, wood, and other substances available from the local environment." He calls them the "absolute poor." It's only reasonable to assume that another billion people will be added to that class, mostly in what are now the less-developed countries, before population growth stabilizes. How will those additional billion, deprived of education and other advantages, interact with the tropical landscape? Not likely by entering information-intensive jobs in the service sector of the new global economy. Julian Simon argued that human ingenuity—and by extension, human population itself—is "the ultimate resource" for solving Earth's problems, transcending Earth's limits, and turning scarcity into abundance. But if all the bright ideas generated by a human population of 5.9 billion haven't yet relieved the desperate needfulness of the 1.1 billion absolute poor, why should we expect that human ingenuity will do any better for roughly 2 billion poor in the future?

Other writers besides Durning have warned about this deepening class rift. Tom Athanasiou, in *Divided Planet: The Ecology of Rich and Poor*, sees population growth only exacerbating the division, and notes that governments often promote destructive schemes of transmigration and rainforest colonization as safety valves for the pressures of land hunger and discontent. A young Canadian policy analyst named Thomas Homer-Dixon, author of several calm-voiced but frightening articles on the linkage between what he terms "environmental scarcity" and global sociopolitical instability, reports that the amount of cropland available per person is falling in the less-developed countries because of population growth and because millions of hectares "are being lost each year to a combination of problems, including encroachment by cities, erosion, depletion of nutrients, acidification, compacting and salinization and waterlogging from overirrigation." In the cropland pinch and other forms of environmental scarcity, Homer-Dixon foresees potential for "a widening gap" of two sorts—between demands on the state and its ability to deliver, and more basically between rich and poor. In conversation with the journalist Robert D. Kaplan, as quoted in Kaplan's book *The Ends of the Earth*, Homer-Dixon said it more vividly: "Think of a stretch limo in the potholed streets of New York City, where homeless beggars live. Inside the limo are the air-conditioned post-industrial regions of North America, Europe, the emerging Pacific Rim, and a few other isolated places, with their trade summitry and computer information highways. Outside is the rest of mankind, going in a completely different direction." That direction, necessarily, will be toward ever more desperate exploitation of landscape. Kaplan himself commented: "We are entering a bifurcated world."

H. G. Wells foretold that bifurcation a century ago in his novel *The Time Machine*. Wells's time traveler, bouncing forward from Victorian London to the year 802,701 A.D., found a divided planet too, upon which the human race had split into two very different forms: the groveling, dangerous Morlocks who lived underground, and the epicene Eloi, who enjoyed lives of languid comfort on the surface. The only quaint thing about Wells's futurology, from where we sit now, is that he imagined it would be necessary to travel so far.

As for Homer-Dixon's vehicle: When you think of that stretch limo on those potholed urban streets, don't assume there will be room inside for tropical forests. Even Noah's ark only managed to rescue paired animals, not large parcels of habitat. The jeopardy of the ecological fragments that we presently cherish as parks, refuges, and reserves is already severe, due to both internal and external forces: internal, because insularity itself leads to ecological unraveling; and external, because those areas are still under siege by needy and covetous people. Projected forward into a future of 10.8 billion humans, of which perhaps 2 billion are starving at the periphery of those areas, while another 2 billion are living in a fool's paradise maintained by unremitting exploitation of whatever resources remain, that jeopardy increases to the point of impossibility. In addition, any form of climate change in the mid-term future, whether caused by greenhouse gases or by the natural flip-flop of climatic forces, is liable to change habitat conditions within a given protected area beyond the tolerance range for many species. If such creatures can't migrate beyond the park or reserve boundaries in order to chase their habitat needs, they may be "protected" from guns and chainsaws within their little island, but they'll still die.

We shouldn't take comfort in assuming that at least Yellowstone National Park will still harbor grizzly bears in the year 2150, that at least Royal Chitwan in Nepal will still harbor tigers, that at least Serengeti in Tanzania and Gir in India will still harbor lions. Those predator populations, and other species down the cascade, are likely to disappear. "Wildness" will be a word applicable only to urban turmoil. Lions, tigers, and bears will exist in zoos, period. Nature won't come to an end, but it will look very different.

The most obvious differences will be those I've already mentioned: Tropical forests and other terrestrial ecosystems will be dramatically reduced in area, and the fragmented remnants will stand tiny and isolated. Because of those two factors, plus the cascading secondary effects, plus an additional dire factor I'll mention in a moment, much of Earth's biological diversity will be gone. How much? That's impossible to predict confidently, but the careful guesses of Robert May, Stuart Pimm, and other biologists suggest losses reaching half to two-thirds of all species. In the oceans, deepwater fish and shellfish populations will be drastically depleted by overharvesting, if not to the point of extinction then at least enough to cause more cascading consequences. Coral reefs and other shallow-water ecosystems will be badly stressed, if not devastated, by erosion and chemical runoff from the land. The additional dire factor is invasive species, fifth of the five factors contributing to our current experiment in mass extinction.

That factor, even more than habitat destruction and fragmentation, is a symptom of modernity. Maybe you haven't heard much about invasive species, but in coming years you will. Daniel Simberloff, the same ecologist who gave that sobering paper that Jablonski remembers from 1983, takes it so seriously that he recently committed himself to founding an institute on invasive biology at the

University of Tennessee, and Interior Secretary Bruce Babbitt sounded the alarm in an April 1998 speech to a weed-management symposium in Denver. The spectacle of a cabinet secretary denouncing an alien plant called purple loosestrife struck some observers as droll, but it wasn't as silly as it seemed. Forty years ago, Charles Elton warned in *The Ecology of Invasions by Animals and Plants* that "we are living in a period of the world's history when the mingling of thousands of kinds of organisms from different parts of the world is setting up terrific dislocations in nature." Elton's word "dislocations" was nicely chosen to ring with a double meaning: Species are being moved from one location to another, and as a result ecosystems are being thrown into disorder.

The problem dates back to when people began using ingenious new modes of conveyance (the horse, the camel, the canoe) to travel quickly across mountains, deserts, and oceans, bringing with them rats, lice, disease microbes, burrs, dogs, pigs, goats, cats, cows, and other forms of parasitic, commensal, or domesticated creature. One immediate result of those travels was a wave of island-bird extinctions, claiming more than a thousand species, that followed oceangoing canoes across the Pacific and elsewhere. Having evolved in insular ecosystems free of predators, many of those species were flightless, unequipped to defend themselves or their eggs against ravenous mammals. *Raphus cucullatus*, a giant cousin of the pigeon lineage, endemic to Mauritius in the Indian Ocean and better known as the dodo, was only the most easily caricatured representative of this much larger pattern. Dutch sailors killed and ate dodos during the seventeenth century, but probably what guaranteed the extinction of *Raphus cucullatus* is that the European ships put ashore rats, pigs, and *Macaca fascicularis*, an opportunistic species of Asian monkey. Although commonly known as the crab-eating macaque, *M. fascicularis* will eat almost anything. The monkeys are still pestilential on Mauritius, hungry and daring and always ready to grab what they can, including raw eggs. But the dodo hasn't been seen since 1662.

The European age of discovery and conquest was also the great age of biogeography—that is, the study of what creatures live where, a branch of biology practiced by attentive travelers such as Carl Linnaeus, Alexander von Humboldt, Charles Darwin, and Alfred Russel Wallace. Darwin and Wallace even made biogeography the basis of their discovery that species, rather than being created and plopped onto Earth by divine magic, evolve in particular locales by the process of natural selection. Ironically, the same trend of far-flung human travel that gave biogeographers their data also began to muddle and nullify those data, by transplanting the most ready and roguish species to new places and thereby delivering misery unto death for many other species. Rats and cats went everywhere, causing havoc in what for millions of years had been sheltered, less competitive ecosystems. The Asiatic chestnut blight and the European starling came to America; the American muskrat and the Chinese mitten crab got to Europe. Sometimes these human-mediated transfers were unintentional, sometimes merely shortsighted. Nostalgic sportsmen in New Zealand imported British red deer; European brown trout and Coastal rainbows were planted in disregard of the native cutthroat trout of Rocky Mountain rivers. Prickly-pear cactus, rabbits, and cane toads were inadvisedly welcomed to Australia. Goats went wild in the Galápagos. The bacteria that cause bubonic plague journeyed from China to Europe by way of fleas, rats, Mongolian horsemen, and sailing ships, and eventually traveled also to California. The Atlantic sea lamprey found its own way up into Lake Erie, but only after the Welland Canal gave it a bypass around Niagara Falls. Unintentional or otherwise, all these transfers had unforeseen consequences, which in many cases included the extinction of less competitive, less opportunistic native species. The rosy wolfsnail, a small creature introduced onto Oahu for the purpose of controlling a larger and more obviously noxious species of snail, which was itself invasive, proved to be medicine worse than the disease; it became a fearsome predator upon native snails, of which twenty species are now gone. The Nile perch, a big predatory fish introduced into Lake Victoria in 1962 because it promised good eating, seems to have exterminated at least eighty species of smaller cichlid fishes that were native to the lake's Mwanza Gulf.

The problem is vastly amplified by modern shipping and air transport, which are quick and capacious enough to allow many more kinds of organism to get themselves transplanted into zones of habitat they never could have reached on their own. The brown tree snake, having hitchhiked aboard military planes from the New Guinea region near the end of World War II, has eaten most of the native forest birds of Guam. The same virus that causes monkeypox among Congolese villagers traveled to Wisconsin by way of certain African rodents, which were imported for the exotic wildlife trade; the virus then crossed into captive American prairie dogs and, from them, into people who thought prairie dogs would make nifty pets. SARS rode from Hong Kong to Toronto as the respiratory distress of one airline passenger. Ebola will next appear who knows where. Apart from the frightening epidemiological possibilities, agricultural damages are the most conspicuous form of impact. One study, by the congressional Office of Technology Assessment, reports that in the United States 4,500 nonnative species have established free-living populations, of which about 15 percent cause severe harm; looking at just 79 of those species, the OTA documented $97 billion in damages. The lost value in Hawaiian snail species or cichlid diversity is harder to measure. But another report, from the U.N. Environmental Program, declares that almost 20 percent of the world's endangered vertebrates suffer from pressures (competition, predation, habitat transformation) created by exotic interlopers. Michael

Soulé, a biologist much respected for his work on landscape conversion and extinction, has said that invasive species may soon surpass habitat loss and fragmentation as the major cause of "ecological disintegration." Having exterminated Guam's avifauna, the brown tree snake has lately been spotted in Hawaii.

Is there a larger pattern to these invasions? What do fire ants, zebra mussels, Asian gypsy moths, tamarisk trees, maleleuca trees, kudzu, Mediterranean fruit flies, boll weevils, and water hyacinths have in common with crab-eating macaques or Nile perch? Answer: They are *weedy* species, in the sense that animals as well as plants can be weedy. What that implies is a constellation of characteristics: They reproduce quickly, disperse widely when given a chance, tolerate a fairly broad range of habitat conditions, take hold in strange places, succeed especially well in disturbed ecosystems, and resist eradication once they're established. They are scrappers, generalists, opportunists. They tend to thrive in human-dominated terrain because in crucial ways they resemble *Homo sapiens*: aggressive, versatile, prolific, and ready to travel. The city pigeon, a cosmopolitan creature derived from wild ancestry as a Eurasian rock dove (*Columba livia*) by way of centuries of pigeon fanciers whose coop-bred birds occasionally went AWOL, is a weed. So are those species that, benefiting from human impacts upon landscape, have increased grossly in abundance or expanded their geographical scope without having to cross an ocean by plane or by boat—for instance, the coyote in New York, the raccoon in Montana, the whitetail deer in northern Wisconsin or western Connecticut. The brown-headed cowbird, also weedy, has enlarged its range from the eastern United States into the agricultural Midwest at the expense of migratory songbirds. In gardening usage the word "weed" may be utterly subjective, indicating any plant you don't happen to like, but in ecological usage it has these firmer meanings. Biologists frequently talk of weedy species, referring to animals as well as plants.

Paleontologists, too, embrace the idea and even the term. Jablonski himself, in a 1991 paper published in *Science*, extrapolated from past mass extinctions to our current one and suggested that human activities are likely to take their heaviest toll on narrowly endemic species, while causing fewer extinctions among those species that are broadly adapted and broadly distributed. "In the face of ongoing habitat alteration and fragmentation," he wrote, "this implies a biota increasingly enriched in widespread, weedy species—rats, ragweed, and cockroaches—relative to the larger number of species that are more vulnerable and potentially more useful to humans as food, medicine, and genetic resources." Now, as we sit in his office, he repeats: "It's just a question of how much the world becomes enriched in these weedy species." Both in print and in talk he uses "enriched" somewhat caustically, knowing that the actual direction of the trend is toward impoverishment of variety.

Regarding impoverishment, let's note another dark, interesting irony: that the two converse trends I've described—partitioning the world's landscape by habitat fragmentation, and unifying the world's landscape by global transport of weedy species—produce not converse results but one redoubled result, the further loss of biological diversity. Immersing myself in the literature of extinctions, and making dilettantish excursions across India, Madagascar, New Guinea, Indonesia, Brazil, Guam, Australia, New Zealand, Wyoming, the hills of Burbank, and other semi-wild places over the past decade, I've seen those redoubling trends everywhere, portending a near-term future in which Earth's landscape is threadbare, leached of diversity, heavy with humans, and "enriched" in weedy species. That's an ugly vision, but I find it vivid. Wildlife will consist of the pigeons and the coyotes and the whitetails, the black rats (*Rattus rattus*) and the brown rats (*Rattus norvegicus*) and a few other species of worldly rodent, the crab-eating macaques and the cockroaches (though, as with the rats, not *every* species—some are narrowly endemic, like the giant Madagascar hissing cockroach) and the mongooses, the house sparrows and the house geckos and the houseflies and the barn cats and the skinny brown feral dogs and a short list of additional species that play by our rules. Forests will be tiny insular patches existing on bare sufferance, much of their biological diversity (the big predators, the migratory birds, the shy creatures that can't tolerate edges, and many other species linked inextricably with those) long since decayed away. They will essentially be tall woody gardens, not forests in the richer sense. Elsewhere the landscape will have its strips and swatches of green, but except on much-poisoned lawns and golf courses the foliage will be infested with cheatgrass and European buckthorn and spotted knapweed and Russian thistle and leafy spurge and salt meadow cordgrass and Bruce Babbitt's purple loosestrife. Having recently passed the great age of biogeography, we will have entered the age *after* biogeography, in that virtually everything will live virtually everywhere, though the list of species that constitute "everything" will be small. I see this world implicitly foretold in the U.N. population projections, the FAO reports on deforestation, the northward advance into Texas of Africanized honeybees, the rhesus monkeys that haunt the parapets of public buildings in New Delhi, and every fat gray squirrel on a bird feeder in England. Earth will be a different sort of place—soon, in just five or six human generations. My label for that place, that time, that apparently unavoidable prospect, is the Planet of Weeds. Its main consoling felicity, as far as I can imagine, is that there will be no shortage of crows.

Now we come to the question of human survival, a matter of some interest to many. We come to a certain fretful leap of logic that other wise thoughtful observers seem willing, even eager, to make: that the ultimate consequence will be the extinction of us. By seizing such a huge share of Earth's landscape, by imposing so wantonly on its providence and presuming so recklessly on its forgiveness, by killing off so many species, they say, we will doom our own species to extinction. This is a commonplace argument among the environmentally exercised. In earlier years, from a somewhat less informed perspective, I've made the same argument myself. Since then, my thinking has changed. My objection to the idea now is that it seems ecologically improbable and too optimistic. But it bears examining, because it's frequently offered as the ultimate argument against proceeding as we are.

Jablonski also has his doubts. Do you see *Homo sapiens* as a likely survivor, I ask him, or as a casualty? "Oh, we've got to be one of the most bomb-proof species on the planet," he says. "We're geographically widespread, we have a pretty remarkable reproductive rate, we're incredibly good at co-opting and monopolizing resources. I think it would take a really serious, concerted effort to wipe out the human species." The point he's making is one that has probably already dawned on you: *Homo sapiens* itself is the consummate weed. Why shouldn't we survive, then, on the Planet of Weeds? But there's a wide range of possible circumstances, Jablonski reminds me, between the extinction of our species and the continued growth of human population, consumption, and comfort. "I think we'll be one of the survivors," he says, "sort of picking through the rubble." Besides losing all the pharmaceutical and genetic resources that lay hidden within those extinguished species, and all the spiritual and aesthetic values they offered, he foresees unpredictable levels of loss in many physical and biochemical functions that ordinarily come as benefits from diverse, robust ecosystems—functions such as cleaning and recirculating air and water, mitigating droughts and floods, decomposing wastes, controlling erosion, creating new soil, pollinating crops, capturing and transporting nutrients, damping short-term temperature extremes and longer-term fluctuations of climate, restraining outbreaks of pestiferous species, and shielding Earth's surface from the full brunt of ultraviolet radiation. Strip away the ecosystems that perform those services, Jablonski says, and you can expect grievous detriment to the reality we inhabit. "A lot of things are going to happen that will make this a crummier place to live—a more stressful place to live, a more difficult place to live, a less resilient place to live—before the human species is at any risk at all." And maybe some of the new difficulties, he adds, will serve as incentive for major changes in the trajectory along which we pursue our aggregate self-interests. Maybe we'll pull back before our current episode matches the Triassic extinction or the K-T event. Maybe it will turn out to be no worse than the Eocene extinction, with a 35 percent loss of species.

"Are you hopeful?" I ask.

Given that hope is a duty from which paleontologists are exempt, I'm surprised when he answers, "Yes, I am."

I'm not. My own guess about the mid-term future, excused by no exemption, is that our Planet of Weeds will indeed be a crummier place, a lonelier and uglier place, and a particularly wretched place for the 2 billion people comprising Alan Durning's absolute poor. What will increase most dramatically as time proceeds, I suspect, won't be generalized misery or futuristic modes of consumption but the gulf between two global classes experiencing those extremes. Progressive failure of ecosystem functions? Yes, but human resourcefulness of the sort Julian Simon so admired will probably find stopgap technological remedies, to be available for a price. So the world's privileged class—that's your class and my class—will probably still manage to maintain themselves inside Homer-Dixon's stretch limo, drinking bottled water and breathing bottled air and eating reasonably healthy food that has become incredibly precious, while the potholes in the road outside grow ever deeper. Eventually the limo will look more like a lunar rover. Ragtag mobs of desperate souls will cling to its bumpers, like groupies on Elvis's final Cadillac. The absolute poor will suffer their lack of ecological privilege in the form of lowered life expectancy, bad health, absence of education, corrosive want, and anger. Maybe in time they'll find ways to gather themselves in localized revolt against the affluent class, and just set to eating them, as Wells's Morlocks ate the Eloi. Not likely, though, as long as affluence buys guns. In any case, well before that they will have burned the last stick of Bornean dipterocarp for firewood and roasted the last lemur, the last grizzly bear, the last elephant left unprotected outside a zoo.

Jablonski has a hundred things to do before leaving for Alaska, so after two hours I clear out. The heat on the sidewalk is fierce, though not nearly as fierce as this summer's heat in New Delhi or Dallas, where people are dying. Since my flight doesn't leave until early evening, I cab downtown and take refuge in a nouveau-Cajun restaurant near the river. Over a beer and jambalaya, I glance again at Jablonski's 1991 *Science* paper, titled "Extinctions: A Paleontological Perspective." I also play back the tape of our conversation, pressing my ear against the little recorder to hear it over the lunch-crowd noise.

Among the last questions I asked Jablonski was, What will happen *after* this mass extinction, assuming it proceeds to a worst-case scenario? If we destroy half or two thirds of all living species, how long will it take for evolution to fill the planet back up? "I don't know the answer to that," he said. "I'd rather not bottom out and see what happens next." In the journal paper he had hazarded that, based on fossil evidence in rock laid down atop the K-T event and others, the time required for full recovery might be 5 or 10 million years. From a paleontological perspective, that's fast. "Biotic recoveries after mass extinctions are geologically rapid but immensely prolonged on human time scales," he wrote. There was also the proviso, cited from another expert, that recovery might not begin until after the extinction-causing circumstances have disappeared. But in this case, of course, the circumstances won't likely disappear until *we* do.

Still, evolution never rests. It's happening right now, in weed patches all over the planet. I'm not presuming to alert you to the end of the world, the end of evolution, or the end of nature. What I've tried to describe here is not an absolute end but a very deep dip, a repeat point within a long, violent cycle. Species die, species arise. The relative pace of those two processes is what matters. Even rats and cockroaches are capable—given the requisite conditions, namely, habitat diversity and time—of speciation. And speciation brings new diversity. So we might reasonably imagine an Earth upon which, 10 million years after the extinction (or, alternatively, the drastic transformation) of *Homo sapiens*, wondrous forests are again filled with wondrous beasts. That's the good news.

PART III

WHAT CAN WE DO?

Can the Ultimate
Rogue Species Be Tamed?

CHAD PEELING

For a biography of Chad Peeling, see the introduction to Chapter 5, page 73.

In "Can the Ultimate Rogue Species Be Tamed?" Peeling invites his reader to examine the behavior of the world's most dangerous invasive species—by looking in the nearest mirror.

My work involves interpreting nature through living exhibits, and I spend a lot of time explaining how the astounding diversity of life on Earth evolved from a common ancestor. A big part of that story involves boundaries. We live in a world of islands—not just those surrounded by water, but islands of habitat bounded by forests, deserts, temperature clines, and other natural barriers. By isolating populations of organisms, habitat islands select for traits that suit local conditions and provide a huge variety of "test tubes" for life's open-ended experimentation. As humans shuttle species between habitat islands we effectively bring down the barriers, destroying the very thing that made biodiversity possible.

Aside from hurricanes and a handful of other natural phenomena, people are the primary vectors of rogue species. One hallmark of humanity is that when we move, we bring along other life forms. As early people migrated across continents and over seas, they brought crops, livestock, and diseases with them. In many cases these species introductions created sweeping environmental disruptions, particularly on islands. As Daniel Simberloff chronicles elsewhere in this book, plant and animal diversity plummeted after humans arrived in Hawaii—to such a degree that paleontologists can pinpoint the arrival of Polynesian settlers in preserved sediments. The sudden disappearance of whole suites of organisms in the sediments coincides with the appearance of human artifacts and the bones of their rogue stowaways—rats, dogs, and pigs. Similar declines in biodiversity occurred after human caravans arrived in the island nations of New Zealand, Australia, and many others.

Viewed in one light, humanity itself is the ultimate rogue species—superadaptable, mobile, and explosively reproductive. Some paleontologists think that the large mammals of pre-human North America—saber-toothed cats, mammoths, giant beavers— were driven to extinction by the newly arrived "hunting apes."

Reasonable people have asked me why invasive species are any different from natural migrations that have occurred throughout life's history. Isn't evolution all about change, anyway? Why single out a few changes we happen to dislike and label these as ecological catastrophes?

It's true that species invasions are not new; what *is* new is the rate of such invasions, along with their global reach. Moving cargo and people around the world daily provides plenty of opportunity for accidental species introductions. Irresponsible gardeners and pet owners have released untold numbers of plants and animals, and the movement of agricultural products is a major source of infection. My office in Pennsylvania has been called to accept South American tarantulas and treefrogs that hitchhiked on fruit shipments and geckos that survived transcontinental shipping with nursery plants. We have also taken in African monitor lizards, tortoises native to Florida, and an Australian emu turned loose by pet owners.

Evolution simply cannot keep pace with the wholesale redistribution of species provided by a global transportation system. Organisms can evolve much faster than once thought, but they still need enough time to accumulate inherited changes over generations. The sudden appearance of an invasive species changes the rules of the evolutionary game, creating a whole new set of selective pressures. Organisms that can adapt quickly survive; those that can't may be driven to extinction. Given enough time, evolution will bring invasive species into some sort of balance and new species will evolve to take advantage of niches left open by extinctions. But this recovery will not happen on a human timescale. From our current perspective, and that of our foreseeable descendants, many of the changes wrought by species invasions are permanent.

As a result, worldwide rogue species exact a huge toll on biodiversity—a toll that, in terms of overall damage, is second only to habitat loss. It's tough to pin down the numbers precisely, but biological invaders have probably contributed to about half of all modern extinctions. Remote islands are particularly susceptible, because indigenous wildlife has evolved without regular influence from outside species. Many far-flung islands also lack big predators or grazing animals, or creatures too large or fragile to be blown or rafted in by natural forces. Isolated from the effects of large predators and stiff competition, islands nurture the evolution of intricate relationships and specializations. Many of the most bizarre creatures on the planet are island specialists. But isolation also leaves islands ecologically naive. Like an infant whose immune system has not been tempered by infection, island ecosystems are wide open to invasion—especially by generalist predators.

The South Pacific island of Guam has become a cautionary tale for the consequences of island invasion. Brown tree snakes accidentally released on Guam just after World War II found the local bird life naive to the possibility that snakes could eat them. Like many islands Guam had no indigenous snakes, so the native wildlife evolved without need of anti-snake behaviors. Amid this dietary windfall, the snakes multiplied quickly and spread across the island. As the snake population grew, the populations of bite-sized birds, lizards, and bats plummeted. More than 80 percent of Guam's native forest birds are now gone. Several species of lizards and one species of bat have also been eaten to extinction, and others are on the brink. The invasion of brown tree snakes has saddled Guam with economic consequences, too. The snakes climb electrical poles and guy wires as easily as they climb trees and vines, and their bodies create short circuits, causing power outages every few days. And by eliminating insect-eating birds the snakes have exposed local agriculture to increased insect damage, and people to disease vectors.

So invasive species pose a danger to ecological diversity that is real, and growing. But what can we do about it?

As with most complex problems, there is no magic-bullet solution for invasive species. Obviously, the ideal scenario would be to prevent any new invasions. But stopping the spread of species entirely would require all-out protectionism—no movement of plants, animals, or their products—not only between continents but between contiguous regions separated by mountain ranges or other natural barriers. This would take an enormous toll on modern life, the global economy, and personal freedom. Would you want to live without bananas, exotic houseplants, imported textiles, and most pets?

Screening people and cargo at national borders can dramatically reduce accidental introductions. Today Australia—home of the cane toad catastrophe—is far ahead of the United States in this regard. Beset by a gaggle of rogue species, Australians have made biosecurity a national policy. Upon entering the country, visitors have to pass through a security checkpoint, where working dogs sniff luggage and people (one nearly mauled my jacket when I forgot to discard a sealed packet of beef jerky). Signs warn of the environmental consequences of biological invasion, and uniformed officers comb through every inch of luggage while quizzing tourists about their recent travels.

We need a sensible legal framework to deal with invasive species, but there is a temptation to lurch too far with regulation. At first blush, it might seem reasonable to prohibit or restrict the ownership, trade, and transport of exotic plants and animals to protect the greater good. But blanketing a complex problem in regulations and bureaucracy is intellectually lazy. It abridges the freedom of responsible citizens and very often misses the real target—fly-by-night companies and unscrupulous individuals who wouldn't bother consulting the law anyway.

As part of our educational outreach program, my office interacts with wildlife permitting agencies in states throughout the United States and Canada. Most of these agencies are over-tasked and under-funded, struggling to enforce impractical laws enacted with good intentions. The result is often inefficiency with little meaningful public benefit. I favor laws that target destructive behavior directly, holding individuals and corporations legally accountable for releasing non-native wildlife. Intentional releases or those caused by negligence should be treated as crimes or, at least, be subject to civil adjudication. The price of freedom is responsibility and vigilance.

Releasing an invasive species is like starting a wildfire, and a similar approach should be used to control both. Society has not banned matches and kindling in the name of fire prevention, and we haven't erected a bureaucracy to issue combustion permits. But we have engaged in widespread public education about fire-related risks and responsibilities (who hasn't heard of Smokey the Bear?); we prosecute arsonists in cases where intent can be proven; and we act quickly to extinguish wildfires as soon as they are discovered. A similar campaign will be needed to control invasive species, based on public education, legal enforcement, and rapid eradication.

Unfortunately, eradicating invasive species is more challenging than putting out wildfires. Simply locating all members of a large animal population requires a serious commitment of time and money. Conservationists on Pinta Island in the Galápagos spent thirty years eradicating 41,000 feral goats. The project began with hunting teams shooting goats on foot. When goats became difficult to find, working dogs tracked them on the paw. And when the dogs could no longer find goats, the last few stragglers were located by leveraging the goats' own gregarious nature. A handful of "Judas" goats, fitted with radio collars, were released on the island. They invariably sought the company of other goats, and hunters were able to follow their radio transmissions to the last remaining individuals.

In addition to goats, conservationists and government agencies have managed to eradicate invasive weeds, rats, pigs, and even fruit flies from a handful of small islands. The techniques developed in these efforts are being applied to other species in other regions.

On continents, rapid eradication is critical before invaders become established over a large area. Burmese pythons from the tropics of Asia have invaded South Florida, and their numbers appear to be growing. There is a reasonable fear among conservationists that these and other tropical snakes could get out of control and decimate South Florida's native birds and mammals. This is a potentially serious invasion in its early stages, and now is the time to marshal an eradication plan. But the response should be proportional to the threat. Concerns that escaped pets might lead to rogue populations in other parts of the country have led to alarmist calls to restrict private ownership of pythons, iguanas and other exotic species. But there is little evidence that these tropical species could survive beyond the extreme southeastern United States. The problems of one region should not be extrapolated to the rest of the continent along with reactionary legislation. All efforts should be directed at eradication.

Yet even this policy is no magic bullet for the rogue species problem. Few people would have a problem with killing invasive rats or pythons, but eradicating goats and other "loveable" mammals brings conservation head-to-head with emotionalism. Animal rights groups halted goat eradication on California's San Clemente Island with a court order while the endangered loggerhead shrike—a bird whose nesting shrubs were being eaten by goats—slipped toward extinction. Imagine the uproar in America if conservationists began systematically eradicating feral dogs and cats, which do tremendous damage by hunting native birds, lizards, mammals, and frogs. We need to value rationalism over emotionalism.

And that leads to the single most important—and perhaps most challenging—part of my prescription. Battling invasive species requires public support, and that requires educating people about the damage inflicted on ecosystems. Under the crush of day-to-day living and bombardment with so many worthy causes, species invasion is not on most people's minds. Rallying public concern takes real work.

It's easy to understand the problem of habitat destruction—we can see the forest being cut or the wetlands being drained. But it's more difficult to understand the seriousness of species invasion, because the effects are subtler and may not impinge on our daily lives. By the time rogue species do affect our daily lives, it's too late for easy solutions.

As I write this, the global human population nears 6.8 billion. No conservation program, law, or government agency can stop the momentum of that many people. The only way to make a lasting impact on invasive species is for citizens to take action, which, in turn, requires that people understand life's diversity and its evolutionary origins. It's high time that we teach evolution in America's science classrooms, museums, and zoological parks, instead of watering down the message to avoid controversy. The concept of evolution is the most important in all of science. It opens windows into the workings of nature and puts humanity in context with the rest of life.

Likewise, biodiversity is one of the most exciting subjects a mind can explore—and I'm convinced that anyone who understands it will care enough to save it.

Government Policy
and the Rogue Species Crisis

CORRY WESTBROOK

Corry Westbrook serves as legislative director for the National Wildlife Federation (NWF) in Washington, DC, helping to set strategy and coordinate outreach to members of Congress on key campaign priorities, including invasive species, public lands and energy policy, climate change legislation, and federal appropriations for wildlife conservation. She first joined NWF in August 2002 as a legislative representative working on endangered species and invasive species policy. She acts as NWF's liaison to the Department of Defense, authored the report *Under Siege: Invasive Species on Military Bases*, and works extensively with coalition partners and the media to raise awareness of legislation that protects wildlife and natural resources. NWF is also a founding member organization of the National Environmental Coalition on Invasive Species, established in 2003.

Before coming to NWF, Corry worked for the National Audubon Society coordinating grassroots outreach for an eight-state region. She has also worked for the Environmental Protection Agency's Office of Ground Water and Drinking Water and the American Indian Environmental Office. In addition, Corry served as a Peace Corps volunteer on the island of Nevis in the West Indies. She has a B.A. in environmental studies, with a minor in biology, from Florida International University and an M.A. from the George Washington University in environmental and natural resource policy.

In "Government Policy and the Rogue Species Crisis," Westbrook outlines what the different levels of government in the U.S. have done and should be doing to address the problems created by invasive species — as well as the ways every concerned citizen can support the cause.

nvasive species are harmful, non-native plants, animals, and microorganisms that are introduced into an environment in which they did not evolve. Usually, they have no natural enemies to limit their reproduction and spread.

The consequences of invasive species for the economy and environment are profound. Exotic invaders comprise the second-largest threat to global biodiversity after habitat loss, threatening 46 percent of species on the Endangered Species Act list. The damages they inflict on agriculture, forestry, fisheries, property, and human health and control costs are estimated at $138 billion annually.[1] For example, controlling the sea lamprey in the Great Lakes costs more than $16 million per year; more than $300 million have been spent since control began nearly sixty years ago. And over the past ten years, $10 billion has been spent as a partial response to address the emerald ash borer.[2]

Climate change is often cited as having an exacerbating effect on the spread of invasive species and the potential damage they cause to native species in both aquatic and terrestrial ecosystems.[3] Scientists expect that many invasive species will gain advantages over native species, facilitated by increased CO_2 concentration, more favorable climate, increased nitrogen deposition, altered disturbance regimes, and increased habitat fragmentation.[4]

International trade, the source of most invasive species infestations, is on the upswing. The problem is therefore urgent and growing—but it does not have to be. We can slow the introduction of new invasive species into the United States.

Real solutions exist that are based on sound science and have bipartisan political support.

The best way to stop new infestations is to stop them from coming into the country in the first place. Once the introduction vectors are shut down, full attention, energy, and money can go to addressing current infestations. But the doors must be shut permanently to new invasive species.

The U.S. government can shut those doors. The major pathways of introduction include the global shipping industry and legal, intentional imports of live plants and animals. When it comes to invasive species, an ounce of prevention is really worth a pound of cure.

Currently the United States lacks an effective legal system to control these means of entry—and to respond rapidly when an invasion occurs. We know how to prevent invasive species from entering the United States, and that action will be cost-effective to the country. Now we just need policy reforms that will allow the federal government, which regulates international trade, to act.

What We've Tried— and Why It Has Failed

Several federal agencies have scattered authority over live, intentionally imported animals. Generally, the U.S. Department of Agriculture (USDA) covers imports that pose risks to livestock and plants, the Center for Disease Control (CDC) covers human disease vectors, and the U.S. Fish and Wildlife Service (FWS) covers all other wildlife, operating under the outdated Lacey Act. This act, which was enacted in 1900, covers a small number of species it has listed as "injurious," mostly birds and mammals. However, its listing system is almost entirely reactive. With limited exceptions, it is not implemented to screen proactively and to prevent new invasions and disease outbreaks,[5] and it is mired in cumbersome regulatory procedures. In short, the current version of the Lacey Act injurious-species listing system does not work to prevent harmful species invasions. On average, it takes more than four years to list a taxon as injurious and prohibit it from import.[6] In one case, seven years passed between the time Congress petitioned FWS to list several species of Asian carp and the agency's 2007 decisions to list three of these—largescale silver carp (*Hypophthalmichthys harmandi*), silver carp (*Hypophthalmichthys molitris*), and black carp (*Mylopharyngodon piceus*).

In 1990 a House Subcommittee requested a report from Congress's former Office of Technology Assessment (OTA) on invasive species. In 1993 the report, entitled *Harmful Non-Indigenous Species in the United States*, was completed. To this day the report, which was produced after a two-year massive study effort, remains an invaluable tool for fully comprehending the scope of the severe challenge this nation faces with respect to invasive species.

The OTA report recommended several policy options to Congress to strengthen national laws for aquatic invasives. However, a decade and a half later, the results have been marginal at best in terms of preventing new imports of harmful aquatic species. In particular, the OTA report emphasized the need to adopt a more stringent and uniform national regulatory policy on prevention of harmful imports. The only progress toward this goal has come from a 1999 Executive Order by President Clinton and the National Invasive Species Council's (NISC) Management Plan of 2001. Both of these lack any new regulatory mandates, are unenforceable, and are routinely ignored by agencies. To have the force of law, a national policy must be adopted by Congress.

For non-native aquatic plants, the situation is as bad as it is for intentionally imported aquatic animals. Risk screening is not required, and the reactive listing approach for federal "noxious weeds" is grossly underfunded and slow. For example, the genus *Caulerpa* is well recognized by marine plant experts as containing numerous aggressive invasive species. One of these species, *C. taxifolia*, an infamous, sea-suffocating Mediterranean invader with the nicknames "marine Astroturf" or "killer algae," has already invaded once in the United States, in Southern California, where it eventually was eradicated after an extremely difficult, multimillion-dollar, underwater fumigation effort.

In April 2003, Defenders of Wildlife filed a detailed petition to USDA, under the petition provisions of the Federal Noxious Weed Act (FNWA), to list the whole *Caulerpa* genus as federal noxious weeds and to broaden the current, very narrow, weed listing for *C. taxifolia*. That petition was endorsed by more than 105 scientists, officials, and others, including the leading national conservation organizations involved with noxious weeds and their impacts.

As of this writing, in 2010, USDA has not yet responded to the *Caulerpa* listing petition, much less actually acted to block the commercial imports of risky species within this genus. Plainly, that agency has given almost no priority to preventing aquatic plant invaders. Unfortunately, by statute, it is the only agency that can prevent international imports of harmful, weedy plants.

In fact, for both Lacey Act animal species listings and FNWA plant listings, the respective agencies—the U.S. Fish and Wildlife Service and USDA—have only one to two full-time employees working on the entire issue. Clearly, more resources must be dedicated to protecting our nation from harmful invasive species.

One of the most important actions Congress can take to fix this problem is to adopt a uniform protective standard to apply to all intentionally imported aquatic species. That protective standard should be as follows:

> Federal agencies shall allow importation of, and interstate commerce in, only those non-native animals and plants that have been assessed by a responsible federal official and determined to pose no or a low likelihood of causing harm to the environment, the economy, public health, or animal or plant health in the United States.

Due to the supremacy of federal laws governing both international and interstate commerce under the Constitution (article one, paragraph eight), states are relatively powerless to impose a "tighter screen" against importation of an aquatic plant or animal species initially allowed into the country under federal law. Further, even if there are stricter laws on the books, no mainland state regularly staffs international entry ports with inspectors seeking to enforce state laws against federally allowed imports. Any given state can do very little to protect itself from a species introduced initially into another state. Moreover, in this age of globalized trade, it is almost impossible for a state to effectively police interstate commerce, as well as the massive, noncommercial, private transportation of aquatic plants and animals, after a potentially harmful species is allowed anywhere inside the nation's borders. In short, governing the importation and interstate movement of non-native species is a distinctly federal function.

As the only entity that can do so, Congress should provide the needed mandate to the federal agencies to follow a new protective standard. It should also provide the relatively modest resources needed to do pre-import screening. Defenders of Wildlife's entire preliminary risk screening effort for 2,241 imported animals required only about four months of work and cost less than $30,000 in staff time and expenses. In the process, it relied on readily accessed scientific and regulatory information, as well as expert opinion, thereby pointing the way to what the federal government can and should, at the bare minimum, do in the future.

Preliminary risk screening is not overly difficult, and it will not only protect our environment and native species but also save the country many millions of dollars in the long run. In sum, our current *laissez-faire* regulatory approach is not cost-effective. Australia, New Zealand, and others do pre-import screening, all in compliance with international law.

Current legislation for addressing invasive species introductions from ballast water has similar problems. Attempts to address ballast water concerns in the United States began with the Nonindigenous Aquatic Nuisance Prevention and Control Act of 1990 (NANPCA),[7] which established a federal program to prevent the introduction and control the spread of unintentionally introduced aquatic nuisance species. The U.S. Coast Guard (USCG), U.S. Environmental Protection Agency (EPA), FWS, Army Corps of Engineers (ACE), and National Oceanic and Atmospheric Administration (NOAA) shared the responsibility for implementing this effort, acting cooperatively as members of an Aquatic Nuisance Species (ANS) Task Force to conduct studies and report to Congress. Under §1101 of NANPCA, a Great Lakes ballast water management (BWM) program (voluntary in its first two years) became mandatory in 1992. This section directed the Coast Guard to issue regulations (33 Code of Federal Regulations, Part 151) to prevent the introduction and spread of aquatic nuisance species into the Great Lakes through the ballast water of vessels. It then established civil and criminal penalties for violating these regulations. NANPCA also encouraged the secretary of Transportation (now the secretary of Homeland Security) to negotiate with foreign countries, through the International Maritime Organization, to prevent and control the unintentional introduction of aquatic nuisance species.[8]

In 1996, the National Invasive Species Act (NISA) amended NANPCA to create a national ballast management program modeled after the Great Lakes program, wherein all ships entering U.S. waters (after operating outside the U.S. Exclusive Economic Zone) are directed to undertake high-seas (i.e., mid-ocean) ballast exchange or alternative measures pre-approved by the Coast Guard as equally or more effective. While not initially enforced on a ship-by-ship basis, this national program was to have become mandatory within three years of the date on which the Coast Guard issued its voluntary guidelines[9] if ships did not show adequate compliance with the program in the absence of enforcement.[10]

The National Ballast Information Clearinghouse (NBIC) was developed jointly by the Coast Guard and the Smithsonian Environmental Research Center to synthesize, analyze, and interpret national data concerning BWM. NBIC found that nationwide compliance with ballast exchange reporting requirements was low, with only 30.4 percent of vessels entering the U.S. Exclusive Economic Zone filing reports with NBIC.[11] In addition, a Coast Guard Report to Congress concluded that reporting compliance was insufficient to allow an accurate assessment of voluntary BWM.[12] On January 6, 2003, the Coast Guard proposed penalties for those who failed to submit BWM reports required by 33 U.S.C. §151 Subpart D for most vessels entering U.S. waters.[13] The Coast Guard published its final regulations on June 14, 2004.

NISA has been criticized as inadequate and faulted for several alleged shortcomings, including agency weakness or delay in implementing some of its provisions.[14] Since NISA exempted most coastwise vessel traffic from ballast water exchange guidelines, vessels traveling short distances between U.S. ports (e.g., from San Francisco Bay, which is highly invaded, to Puget Sound, which is less so) are exempt from controls. Others are critical of the provisions of 16 U.S.C. §4711(k)(2)(A), which give the vessel owner a blanket exemption to ignore any mandatory regulations if the vessel's master/captain determines that the vessel might not be able to safely conduct a ballast water exchange on the open ocean. Whereas earlier provisions applicable to the Great Lakes provided a safety exemption, the master/captain of a vessel was required to report the problem to the Coast Guard and conduct alternate BWM measures, often negotiated on a case-by-case basis. Critics believe that the NISA language has eliminated any incentive to change ballast water piping systems or adopt other management or treatment options to deal with the problem safely. Finally, NISA has been criticized for its apparent failure to actually prevent additional introductions of damaging organisms into the Great Lakes, despite this being the one area where the requirements for managing ballast water have been the most stringent for the longest time.[15]

THE PROBLEMS—AND THE SOLUTIONS
Imported Animals

It is easy to provide numerous case studies of harmful invaders, but is there an accounting of the intentional and legal importation of animals into the United States? In fact, the first comprehensive assessment of all the animal species intentionally and legally imported into the country—and the risks they pose—is contained in a report by Defenders of Wildlife titled "Broken Screens: The Regulation of Live Animal Imports in the United States."[16] Following is a brief summary of its key findings on aquatic animal imports:

- Although many imported species are not identified to species level in the public records, it can be confidently stated that about 900 different, identified non-native, aquatic species (vertebrate and invertebrate) were imported from 2000 through 2004, representing close to 1 billion individual organisms, primarily tropical fish.
- Preliminary risk screening found that over 80 of those 900 imported species (or about 9 percent) presented potential risks of becoming invasive species and/or spreading disease, according to readily accessible scientific sources. A more detailed screening would undoubtedly find even more risky species.

Here are just a few examples of the dangerous animal species that have been imported into the United States and the risks they pose:

- The snakehead fish (Family *Channa*) is a voracious predator that was imported from Asia for the specialty food market and then released surreptitiously into natural waterways. Snakeheads are disrupting the ecology of the Potomac River and spreading. Imports were retroactively banned under the current Lacey Act, but the ban came far too late to stop this invasion.
- The red lionfish (*Pterois volitans*) is an aggressive, poison-spined, tropical pet fish originating from Indo-Pacific areas. It has formed wild populations off the Atlantic coast, where it stings divers and fishers and harms native marine species as well. This is the first documented establishment of a non-native marine fish thought to have originated via private pet fish releases.
- A famous example of an intentional non-aquatic animal import is the Gambian rat (*Cricetomys gambianus*). It was in a shipment of giant Gambian rats brought in for the pet trade that monkeypox, an animal disease, was introduced into the United States. This disease affects mainly rodents, but humans are also susceptible. Spread mostly through infected pet prairie dogs that were exposed to the African rodents, monkeypox sickened approximately eighty people in six states in 2003. If it were to infect native prairie dogs, the disease could decimate populations of native U.S. species and make them permanent reservoirs for the virus.

The solution: Pass new legislation that allows the import only of those non-native animal species that have first been evaluated and screened based on any risks they present to human health, animal health, or the environment.

Imported Plants

As with animals, there is a long list of dangerous plant species and diseases that have been introduced into the United States. Here are a few examples:

- Beach vitex (*Vitex rotundifolia*) is a woody vine native to the Pacific Rim. In the 1980s, it was imported and planted on Carolina beaches to help stabilize dunes. It proved better at crowding out native vegetation than at holding dunes in place. By 2003, beach vitex was infringing on the nesting habitat of loggerhead sea turtles and had earned the nickname "the kudzu of the Carolina coast." Despite five years of control, beach vitex continues to spread and was recently spotted in Virginia.

- Brazilian pepper (*Schinus terebinthifolius*), melaleuca, and hydrilla were introduced into Florida for various reasons in the 1900s. Since their introduction, these plants and many others have caused severe problems in the state. In fiscal year 1999–2000, nine Florida agencies spent $90.8 million on prevention, monitoring, control, and restoration efforts. The annual cost of invasive plants, animals, and diseases in terms of losses to Florida's agriculture is estimated at $179 million.

- Sudden oak death (*Phytophthora ramorum*) is a plant disease that is suspected to have been imported, unnoticed, through infected woody nursery plants. This fungus has killed more than a million trees in California. Since 2004, West Coast nurseries shipped infected plants to states across the country—where dozens of species of native oaks and shrubs are vulnerable.

The solution: Implement a pre-import screening system to assess the invasion and weediness risks of non-native plants before they are imported into the nursery or aquarium trade, with provisions to keep out those plants deemed most risky. Adopt stronger national and international rules to ensure that plants in trade are free of pests and diseases.

Organisms in Ships' Ballast Water

Species that enter the United States not through intentional importing but as "stowaways" in the ballast water carried by ocean-going ships can pose an enormous, often unrecognized threat to existing ecosystems. Some examples:

- The veined rapa whelk (*Rapana venosa*) is a large, predatory marine snail native to the Sea of Japan. Likely introduced to the lower Chesapeake Bay via ballast water, the snail eats oysters, clams, and mussels. It is deemed a potential threat to clam and oyster populations in the lower Chesapeake, which already are at very low levels.
- The fishhook waterflea (*Bythotrephes cederstroemi*), first detected in 1998, was transported to the Great Lakes from northeastern Europe in the ballast tanks of commercial ships. This occurred following the first-ever measures enacted to protect the Great Lakes—an objective these measures proved too weak to achieve. Like other freshwater invaders first introduced to the Great Lakes, water fleas are likely to spread across America, placing fishing resources at risk throughout the coun-

try. They reproduce rapidly and compete with juvenile fish for food.

- Zebra mussels (*Dreissena polymorpha*) invaded Lake St. Clair in the late 1980s, probably by hitchhiking in the ballast water of ships. Within a few years, they were abundant enough to clog and temporarily shut down the water supply of Monroe, Michigan. Power plants, water treatment facilities, and factories in New York, Ohio, and Michigan faced drastic reductions in water intake. Between 1978 and 2000, the total damages caused were estimated at $750 million to $1 billion. In the past year, infestations of zebra and quagga mussels into the Great Lakes have spread across the Rocky Mountain divide and into the western states of Nevada and California.

The solution: Enact effective laws and regulations to require that ballast water be treated before it is discharged to a standard that protects the environment and thus stops future invasions.

A National Approach to Managing the Invasive Species Threat

The impacts of invasive species go well beyond a local site or a single state. Countless expert reports from public and private groups have brought attention to these impacts and called for federal action to address invasive species problems. To date, progress has been woefully inadequate. However, there *are* opportunities to act. Here are some specific measures for Congress and the president to take that will turn the solutions we've suggested into specific and successful policy:

Create a comprehensive national system for screening
intentional imports of plant and animal species.

It is extremely difficult and costly to control invasive species once they become established. The best defense is to screen out potential invaders from imports in the first place. Right now, the United States does not require that living organisms being proposed for import be screened for invasiveness beforehand. The need for, and importance of, such a risk screening process has been noted in every major report on invasive species policy for nearly twenty years. In fact, development of such a screening process was a high priority in the 2001 National Invasive Species Management Plan issued by the National Invasive Species Council. Some federal agencies have the statutory authority to implement pre-screening measures, but they have not made it a priority. President Obama needs to direct these agencies to begin pre-import screening immediately. In addition, Congress needs to extend statutory authority to the U.S. Fish and Wildlife Service, as this agency lacks the legal authority to screen many types of animal imports.

Revise the Lacey Act to require
screening of animal imports.

The Lacey Act provides authority for the U.S. Fish and Wildlife Service to name groups of animals as "injurious species" and thereby restrict their import. However, the act does not require that animal species being proposed for import be screened first for either invasiveness or disease risk. This creates unacceptable threats to native wildlife, to the economy, and to human and animal health. Thus, Congress should provide FWS with the necessary authority to screen invasive animals, both terrestrial and aquatic, rather than relying on the Lacey Act's currently ineffective provisions.

If enacted, a recent bill, the Non-native Wildlife Invasion Prevention Act (H.R. 669), would prevent the introduction of non-native wildlife species that pose excessive risk to the economy, the environment, human health, or native wildlife. Specifically, this act would (1) require FWS to assess the potential risks associated with a species proposed for import before deciding whether to allow or prohibit the species and (2) establish a comprehensive law regulating non-native wildlife that would keep potentially harmful animals out in the first place.

Indeed, H.R. 669 would be one of the most important U.S. policy advances ever made in terms of blocking current imports of harmful invasive species—such as the Burmese python and anaconda. Similar legislation is expected to be introduced in the Senate in the 111th Congress.

Speed up and strengthen the
U.S. Department of Agriculture's revision
of plant regulations to screen out weedy imports.

Intentional horticultural and nursery imports are the primary means by which harmful weeds are introduced. Other nations have significantly reduced weedy introductions—and have reaped major economic benefits—by adopting risk screening protocols. The United States urgently needs a similar approach. The USDA's Animal and Plant Health inspection Service (APHIS) needs to promptly revise its regulations for importing plants. These regulations are collectively known as Quarantine 37, or "Q-37."

The Obama administration is already taking positive action. On July 23, 2009, the Department of Agriculture published a proposed rule in the *Federal Register* with revisions to Q-37 import regulations. The main component of the proposal is the strongly supported creation of the new category of "not authorized [for import] pending pest risk analysis" (NAPPRA). This can be an important step toward a prevention system adequate to meet the challenges of the twenty-first century. The hope is that the regulatory revisions in the proposal will be improved as well as quickly adopted and implemented.

Preventing unintentional introductions poses a different but equally important set of challenges. The United States loses hundreds of millions of dollars annually due to aquatic invaders, a direct result of the reactive instead of proactive nature of U.S. policies. We have cost-effective technologies to keep harmful species out of our waters—but what we lack so far is the political will to put these technologies to use.

Reauthorize the National Invasive Species Act and pass a Ballast Water Management Act.

Ballast water is the primary vector for unintentionally introducing invasive aquatic organisms into U.S. waters. An important step in addressing this problem would be to enact and implement new legislation requiring all ships to treat their ballast water before it is discharged and to use specific "best management practices" to stop the continued introduction of aquatic invasive species. New laws would also help coordinate federal and state authority to rapidly respond to new aquatic invasions. Once such legislation is enacted, the U.S. Coast Guard and EPA should assign a top priority to its implementation and enforcement.

The Obama administration has already taken steps to shut down this vector. On August 28, 2009, the Coast Guard published a notice of proposed rulemaking in the *Federal Register*. The administration's aim is to amend the Coast Guard's regulations on ballast water management to reduce the chances of invasive species introductions via ballast water. The proposal includes positive provisions (e.g., a strong final standard for ballast water discharges) but also weak provisions (e.g., overly long time-lines for applying treatment technology), that need to be strengthened before the rule goes final. Overall, however, it is a great first step for a problem that has been neglected for far too long.

Revise the USDA's Q-37 "Plants for Planting" regulations to block plant pests and diseases.

Horticultural introductions (imported plants, cuttings, seeds, etc.) are the principal pathway for introduction of plant pests and diseases that are causing severe ecological and economic damage to American agriculture and forests. As part of its revisions to the Q-37 regulations, the federal government needs to strengthen specific measures to prevent further introductions of devastating plant diseases as well as insects and other plant pests.

The current administration is already taking positive action. On July 23, 2009, the Department of Agriculture published a proposed rule in the *Federal Register* with revisions to Q-37 import regulations. The main component of the proposal is the strongly supported creation of the new category of NAPPRA. In addition to this component, however, all regulations, screening practices, and inspections should be structured to encourage importers to use lower-risk plant materials such as seeds, cuttings, and tissue cultures, which are much less likely to carry plant pests. Mandatory disinfection of all incoming live plants should also be considered.

Increase funding for early detection and rapid response.

When prevention fails, we need to respond swiftly to new invaders. Every delay adds costs and lowers our chances of success. Inadequate funding is penny-wise and pound-foolish. Finding new invaders quickly, and responding rapidly to address them, is essential to limiting impacts and costs in instances of failed prevention. However, agencies often lack the resources for quick responses, a situation that leads to work delays, allows invaders time to spread, and undermines the efforts of the agencies themselves.

Establish an Invasive Species Emergency Fund.

Setting aside special funds—much like those used for responding to oil spills—would permit agencies to respond rapidly to invaders, especially aquatic and insect species, when they are first detected in the country and can be most easily and cheaply addressed.

Fund strategic regional efforts on the ground.

In cases where invasive species are not eliminated immediately, funding for major efforts is essential before they spread throughout the nation. Funding should be prioritized for projects that stop their proliferation into new areas.

Fund a national network
of regional invasive plant agencies.

Agencies focusing on the problem of invasive plant species have developed in many parts of the country, serving as information hubs for natural resource managers on the ground. Networking these agencies into a virtual national center would strengthen the nation's ability to identify and respond to new invasions.

Fill other funding gaps.

Invasive species prevention pays for itself many times over. Agencies currently lack the resources to expedite urgently needed regulatory changes. Increased funding would allow them to better manage widespread invaders, more aggressively address the worst infestations, and better protect valuable natural resources. Addressing the existing funding gaps is especially important given the value of the resources at risk. Economic studies, including detailed analyses by the Brookings Institution, independent economists, and the former congressional Office of Technology Assessment, show that government funds spent on invasive species prevention and control efforts are highly likely to provide large net economic returns to the nation.

Strengthen federal leadership in dealing with invasive species.

We face different challenges for animals, plants, and diseases, but clear opportunities exist for reforms in each area. And stronger federal leadership would transform our invasive species policy for the better overall.

The National Invasive Species Council (NISC) was established by Executive Order 13112 to coordinate invasive species–related actions among several departments and agencies. NISC is co-chaired by the USDA and the Department of the Interior. Other members are the U.S. Departments of Commerce, Defense, Health and Human Services, Homeland Security, State, Transportation, and Treasury, plus the Environmental Protection Agency, the National Aeronautics and Space Administration, the Office of the Trade Representative, and the U.S. Agency for International Development. NISC was also tasked with creating and implementing the National Invasive Species Management Plan. Its first

Management Plan in 2001 was well received, but NISC's effectiveness has been far less than hoped for since then—owing in part to a lack of statutory authority, an unclear role with respect to other federal agencies, and limited funding.

The Obama administration should reinvigorate NISC by ensuring that appointees in the thirteen participating agencies show an exceptional commitment to fulfilling the goals of the Executive Order and Management Plan. In addition, NISC itself should be elevated to a status that gives it independent funding and a level of authority comparable to that of the Council on Environmental Quality, so that it can better oversee, coordinate, and assist agencies in addressing invasive species.

RESPONDING TO THE OPPOSITION

Many regulated industries claim that regulations and new laws are just not necessary—that the problem is not that big. Bear in mind, however, that hundreds of millions of animals are imported each year into the United States with little oversight and at significant risk to people, native species, the environment, and economic activity. The current system for restricting the importation of problematic species (the Lacey Act) takes years and typically occurs only after substantial damage has been done. H.R. 669 would prevent harmful species from entering the country in the first place, taking a proactive approach to protecting our nation's resources and public health. Also, it would ensure that imported organisms are properly and scientifically identified.[17]

Many regulated industries also claim that all nonnative species will be banned. However, H.R. 669 does not ban any species *per se*; rather, it establishes a science-based process for analyzing animal imports with respect to their likelihood to cause harm to our economy, our health, our environment, or other animals. The evaluation process put in place by H.R. 669 will prevent the importation only of those species that are judged to be a serious risk. Further, the bill requires that this process be transparent and that stakeholder input be considered in decisionmaking.

Some regulated industries, such as pet shops and exotic pet dealers, claim that pets will be taken away or possibly killed. But, in fact, any decisions made to prohibit species' import will not affect current pets or domesticated animals. Under H.R. 669 all current pets, even those species that cannot be imported in the future, may be kept by their owners. (See section 3[f] of the bill for more details.) Domesticated animals, including those listed in Section 14 (e.g., dogs, cats, rabbits, horses, goldfish, and others identified by the U.S. Fish and Wildlife Service), would be exempt from the risk analysis process.

Other regulated industries claim that H.R 669 will appropriate excessive amounts of taxpayer dollars to fund the U.S. Fish and Wildlife Service. However, H.R. 669 does not include a specific appropriation for implementation of this program by FWS. Instead, it authorizes the establishment of a fund to pay for the program partly through fees that FWS could charge applicants who recommend species to be evaluated for importation. Congressional decisions to spend taxpayer money to fund federal agencies are made through an annual appropriations process, which is separate from consideration of this bill. And, in any case, the costs of not acting would be greater; without legislation like H.R. 669 to prevent the introduction of invasive and harmful species into the country, the nation would spend even more money controlling these species—costs that already total tens of millions of dollars per year.

Another claim is that the bill will not only shut down the pet industry overnight, costing jobs and hurting the economy, but also stop the work of zoos, aquariums, and research institutions. But, in fact, much of the pet trade will be unaffected by H.R. 669; further, the evaluation process it creates will take more than three years to come into effect, allowing the industry time to adjust. H.R. 669 would have no impact on the trade in domesticated animals, including cats, dogs, and so on. Moreover, the bill includes a list of animals that are exempt—a list that FWS can expand. Any non-native wild animal species could continue to be imported and traded if it was evaluated and found, after stakeholder and public input, not to pose threats to people, native species, the economy, or the environment. And accredited zoos and aquariums, as well as research and educational institutions, would be able to acquire special permits to hold species that are otherwise not approved for import.

With regard to reducing unintentional aquatic invasive species introductions from ballast water, the shipping industry has stated that it is willing to add treatment technology to its ships. In previous years, the shipping industry had opposed ballast water legislation in Congress unless the legislation pre-empted state and Clean Water Act (CWA) authority. Through this pre-emption it was hoping to avoid a patchwork of state regulations as well as citizen suit litigation. However, the shipping industry seemed to recognize the damage done by its depositing of biological pollution into U.S. waters. The Obama administration's proposed rulemaking partly supersedes the need for congressional legislation at this time.

Although estimates of the costs of ballast treatment are imprecise and may vary from vessel to vessel, there is some agreement on average costs.[18] Generally, the cost of retrofitting vessels to treat ballast water has been estimated at between $200,000 and $310,000 per vessel for mechanical treatment and at around $300,000 for chemical treatment.[19] Most of this expense will probably be borne by foreign shipping companies, since the U.S. flag fleet comprises only a small percentage of the global fleet.[20] The likelihood of compliance by the foreign flag fleet was increased in February 2004 by an international agreement on ballast water management.

What Can You Do?

- For information about the latest legislation or administration action regarding invasive species, go to www.necis.net or become a member of the National Wildlife Federation and take direct action through www.nwf.org/action.
- Contact your members of Congress regarding legislation through e-mail, phone calls, letters, or in-district meetings.
- Contact the Obama administration by sending a letter to the White House or to heads of agencies such as the EPA, Department of the Interior, Coast Guard, and APHIS.
- Join local conservation organizations that work to prevent and remove local invasive species infestations.
- Spread the word. Educate your neighbors regarding the invasive species problem, and ask them to take action such as writing letters to the local newspaper and contacting lawmakers.
- Engage the media to showcase the views and opinions of elected officials' constituencies and to educate your community about invasive species problems. Ways to engage the media include editorial meetings, opinion pieces, letters to the editor, phone calls, and in-person meetings.

Twenty-One Simple Things Everyone Can Do to Help Control Rogue Species

We can all play a role in helping to prevent invasive species from damaging our local ecosystems. The following ideas are adapted from the informational website on invasive species maintained by the U.S. Fish and Wildlife Service. More information can be obtained at http://www.fws.gov/invasives/what-you-can-do.html.

1. Find out what the most troublesome invasive species are in your local area, avoid spreading them, and try to control them if you have them on your property.

2. Remember that the seeds of invasive plants can easily get transported in mud and dirt. Always clean the dirt out of your hiking boots or off of your vehicle before you leave an area.

3. Find out who can give guidance about, and identify, unknown species in your area.

4. Don't bring animals, plants, and agricultural products (fruits, vegetables, soil) into the country illegally. Fill out customs declaration forms completely and honestly.

5. Learn more about your local natural areas and the species in your yard. This will help you identify animals and plants that are not native and might be invasive.

6. To the degree possible, use only native plants that are appropriate for your region when you are gardening. Ask your local nursery to start carrying more native plants. Use exotic ornamentals only if you cannot find native alternatives and you are sure the ornamentals are noninvasive.

7. Clean construction machines before moving to a new job site. The mud and soil stuck to the machines can harbor seeds from invasive plants.

8. Try to avoid disturbing natural areas whenever possible. Disturbing natural areas can increase their susceptibility to invasion by exotic species.

9. Help out in your community. Join a local native plant organization or native fish or wildlife group.

10. Ask for only noninvasive species when you acquire plants. Plant only environmentally safe species in your gardens. Work toward and promote new landscape designs that are friendly to regional ecosystems.

11. Seek information on which species are invasive in your area. Sources could include botanical gardens, horticulturists, conservationists, and government agencies. Remove invasive species from your land and replace them with noninvasive species suited to your site and needs.

12. Do not trade plants with other gardeners if you know they are species with invasive characteristics.

13. Request that botanical gardens and nurseries promote, display, and sell only noninvasive species.

14. Help educate your community and other gardeners in your area through personal contact and in such settings as garden clubs and other civic groups.

15. Ask garden writers and other media to emphasize the

problem of invasive species and provide information. Request that garden writers promote only noninvasive species.

16. Invite speakers knowledgeable about the invasive species issue to speak to garden clubs, master gardeners, schools, and other community groups.

17. Seek the best information on control of invasive plant species, and organize neighborhood work groups to remove invasive plant species under the guidance of knowledgeable professionals.

18. Volunteer at botanical gardens and natural areas to assist ongoing efforts to diminish the threat of invasive plants.

19. Participate in early-warning systems by reporting invasive species that you observe in your area. Determine which group or agency should be responsible for reports emanating from your area. If no 800 number exists for such reporting, request that one be established, citing the need for a clearinghouse with an 800 number and website links to information about invasive plant species.

20. Assist garden clubs to create policies regarding the use of invasive species not only in horticulture but also in activities such as flower shows. Urge florists and others to eliminate the use of invasive plant material.

21. Learn more! Become more educated and help spread the word about invasive species.

TO LEARN MORE

Books, Websites, and Organizations
Devoted to Invasive Species and
Our Planet's Endangered Ecosystems

BOOKS

Baskin, Yvonne. *A Plague of Rats and Rubbervines: The Growing Threat of Species Invasions.* Washington, DC: Island Press, 2003.

Widely published science writer Yvonne Baskin draws on extensive research to provide an engaging and authoritative overview of the problem of invasive alien species. She takes the reader on a worldwide tour of grasslands, gardens, waterways, and forests, describing the troubles caused by exotic organisms that run amok in new settings and examining how commerce and travel on an increasingly connected planet are exacerbating this oldest of human-created problems.

Burdick, Alan. *Out of Eden: An Odyssey of Ecological Invasion.* New York: Farrar, Straus and Giroux, 2006.

An exceptionally well-written popular description of the invasive species dilemma and the efforts scientists are making to understand and cope with it. According to *Booklist*: "'Invasion biology' inspired science-journalist Burdick to accompany biologists on their rounds as they assess the problem. Pausing to consider how we view new arrivals, Burdick describes in fine detail the scientists' field and lab work in the places he visited: Guam, the Hawaiian Islands, San Francisco Bay, Chesapeake Bay, and Tasmania. Interspersing biographical sketches of his guides, Burdick's narrative balances the particular problems posed by invading organisms with scientific theories about their ecology."

Carlton, James, and Gregory M. Ruiz, eds. *Invasive Species: Vectors and Management Strategies.* Washington, DC: Island Press, 2003.

"Vectors" are the mechanisms by which invasive species manage to overcome natural obstacles and make their way into new habitats. This book brings together in a single volume current information from leading scientists around the world on approaches to controlling and managing invasion vectors. It serves as a timely and essential reference for scientists, researchers, policymakers, and anyone concerned with understanding biological invasions and developing effective responses to them.

Coates, Peter. *American Perceptions of Immigrant and Invasive Species: Strangers on the Land*. Berkeley: University of California Press, 2007.

Charting shifting attitudes to alien species since the 1850s, Peter Coates brings to light the rich cultural and historical aspects of the invasive species story by situating the history of immigrant flora and fauna within the wider context of human immigration. Through accounts of an illuminating series of particular invasives, including the English sparrow and the eucalyptus tree, Coates shows that we have always perceived plants and animals in relation to ourselves and the polities to which we belong.

Elton, Charles S. *The Ecology of Invasions by Animals and Plants*. Chicago: University of Chicago Press, 2000.

Authored by one of the founders of the modern science of ecology, this classic book (originally published in 1958) sounded an early warning about invasive species. Elton explains, in clear, concise language and with numerous examples, the devastating effects that invasive species can have on local ecosystems. The first book on invasion biology and still the most frequently cited, Elton's masterpiece provides an accessible, engaging introduction to the topic.

Lockwood, Julie, Martha Hoopes, and Michael Marchetti. *Invasion Ecology*. Oxford: Blackwell Publishing, 2007.

Highlighting important research findings associated with each stage of invasion, *Invasion Ecology* provides an overview of the invasion process from transportation patterns and causes of establishment success to ecological impacts, invader management, and post-invasion evolution. This book serves as both a synthesis of current research into invasive species and a useful text for undergraduate and graduate students in ecology and conservation management.

McNeeley, Jeffrey A. *The Great Reshuffling: Human Dimensions of Invasive Alien Species.* Gland, Switzerland: World Conservation Union (IUCN), 2000.

While the issue of invasive alien species has important biological components, the human dimensions deserve much greater attention, since humans, with all their diversity of quirks, strengths, and weaknesses, are at the heart of the problem and, paradoxically, also at the heart of the solution. This compilation of papers delivered during a workshop held in Cape Town, South Africa, in 2000 covers some of the many causes, consequences, and responses to this problem.

Simberloff, Daniel, ed. *Strangers in Paradise: Impact and Management of Nonindigenous Species in Florida.* Washington, DC: Island Press, 1997.

The state of Florida has one of the most severe exotic species problems in the country; as many as a quarter of species in Florida are non-native, and millions of acres of land and water are dominated by nonindigenous species. *Strangers in Paradise* was the first book to address the issue of invasive species in relation to a large, diverse region and the full range of nonindigenous species, the problems they cause, and the methods of and impediments to dealing with them.

Terrill, Ceiridwen. *Unnatural Landscapes: Tracking Invasive Species.* Tucson: University of Arizona Press, 2007.

Traveling by kayak, Ceiridwen Terrill brings readers on a firsthand tour of various "islands" in the southwestern United States and Mexico (actual islands as well as self-contained habitat communities), taking an in-depth look at the damage that invasive species cause. Drawing on field observations, research, and interviews with scientists, resource managers, and local residents, this book provides readers with the background and knowledge they need to understand the threat that invasions pose to fragile ecosystems, especially in the American Southwest.

Van Driesche, Jason, and Roy Van Driesche. *Nature Out of Place: Biological Invasions in the Global Age.* Washington, DC: Island Press, 2004.

The father-and-son team of Jason and Roy Van Driesche offers a unique combination of narratives that highlight both the damage done by invasive species and the underlying scientific and policy issues that relate to managing them. Chapters examine Hawaii, where introduced feral pigs are destroying the islands' native forests; zebra mussel invasions in the rivers of Ohio; and the decades-long effort to eradicate an invasive weed on the Great Plains. The book ends with a number of specific suggestions for ways that individuals can help reduce the impacts of invasive species; it also offers resources for further information.

WEBSITES AND ORGANIZATIONS

Alliance for Global Conservation

http://www.actforconservation.org/

Dedicated to combating global species loss, the Alliance for Global Conservation is a partnership among Conservation International, The Pew Charitable Trusts, The Nature Conservancy, Wildlife Conservation Society, and World Wildlife Fund. The Alliance is working with the U.S. Congress to pass legislation to address extinction and natural resource depletion worldwide.

Center for Invasive Species Research (CISR)

http://cisr.ucr.edu/

CISR supports research into managing the economic, ecological, and sociological effects of exotic pest introductions and other invasive species in California, as well as more broadly examining scientific issues related to the biological underpinnings of the well-being of the burgeoning demography of California.

Defenders of Wildlife

http://www.defenders.org/index.php

Founded in 1947 as Defenders of Furbearers, Defenders of Wildlife now employs over 150 dedicated professionals and is supported by more than 500,000 members nationwide in its mission of preserving our nation's native wildlife species and habitats.

Endangered Species Coalition (ESC)

http://www.stopextinction.org/

ESC is a national network of hundreds of conservation, scientific, education, religious, sporting, outdoor recreation, business, and community organizations working to protect the United States' disappearing wildlife and its last remaining wild places through education, outreach, and especially grassroots organizing, mobilizing citizens to participate in the democratic political process with the goal of protecting endangered species and their habitats.

Global Invasive Species Database (GISD)

http://www.issg.org/database/welcome

Managed by the Invasive Species Specialist Group of the Species Survival Commission of the IUCN–World Conservation Union, GISD focuses on invasive alien species that threaten native biodiversity and covers all taxonomic groups from micro-organisms to animals and plants in all ecosystems.

Global Invasive Species Programme (GISP)

http://www.gisp.org/

GISP is an international partnership established in response to the first international meeting on invasive alien species held in Trondheim, Norway, in 1996. It provides support to the implementation of Article 8(h) of the Convention on Biological Diversity (which calls for preventing "the introduction, control, or eradication of those alien species which threaten ecosystems, habitats or species"). GISP has also contributed extensively to the knowledge and awareness of invasive species through the development of a range of products and publications, including the Global Strategy on Invasive Alien Species and *Invasive Alien Species: A Toolkit of Best Prevention and Management Practices.*

International Fund for Animal Welfare (IFAW)

http://www.ifaw.org/

Beginning with its campaign to protect harp seals from hunting, IFAW has grown to become the world's leading international animal welfare organization. IFAW begins its fourth decade of operation with teams of experienced and dedicated campaigners, legal and political experts, and scientists working from offices in countries around the world.

International Union for the Conservation of Nature (IUCN)
http://www.iucn.org/

IUCN is the world's oldest and largest global environmental network, a democratic membership union with more than 1,000 government and NGO member organizations and almost 11,000 volunteer scientists in more than 160 countries. IUCN's Invasive Species Specialist Group (http://www.issg.org/index.html) is a global network of scientific and policy experts on invasive species that currently has 196 core members from more than 40 countries and a wide informal global network of over 2,000 conservation practitioners and experts who contribute to its work.

Invasive Species Plant Workshop (ISPW)
http://www.centerforplantconservation.org/invasives/invasives.asp

Hosted by the Missouri Botanical Garden and maintained by the Center for Plant Conservation, this site provides a collection of resources and information about invasives that is searchable by state or by topic.

Lady Bird Johnson Wildflower Center
http://wildflower.org/

Former first lady Lady Bird Johnson and actress Helen Hayes founded the center in 1982 to protect and preserve North America's native plants and natural landscapes by introducing people to the beauty and diversity of wildflowers and other native plants. In 2006, the Center became an Organized Research Unit of the University of Texas at Austin.

National Audubon Society
http://www.audubon.org/

The National Audubon Society's mission is to conserve and restore natural ecosystems, focusing on birds, other wildlife, and their habitats for the benefit of humanity and the earth's biological diversity. Audubon's national network of community-based nature centers and chapters, scientific and educational programs, and advocacy on behalf of areas sustaining important bird populations are designed to engage millions of people of all ages and backgrounds in positive conservation experiences. Audubon's Stop Invasives program (http://www.stopinvasives.org/) provides education and advocates legislative action to deal with the problems posed by invasive species.

National Environmental Coalition on Invasive Species (NECIS)
http://www.necis.net/

Established in 2003, NECIS is a national partnership of fifteen major environmental organizations that provides a united expert and scientific voice on invasive species policy. Its leaders include scientists, lawyers, activists, and advocates with many years of experience on invasives policy.

TRAFFIC
http://www.traffic.org/

Founded in 1976, TRAFFIC is a global wildlife trade monitoring network that works to ensure that trade in wild plants and animals is not a threat to the conservation of nature. Research-driven and action-oriented, it is committed to delivering innovative and practical conservation solutions based on the latest information, and maintains nine regional programs coordinated by the international headquarters in Cambridge, U.K.

U.S. Fish and Wildlife Service
http://www.fws.gov/invasives/index.html

The only agency of the U.S. government whose primary responsibility is the conservation of the nation's fish, wildlife, and plants, the U.S. Fish and Wildlife Service website contains an extensive collection of information resources about invasive species, including news about trends, laws and regulations, and educational programs, as well as useful tips and guidance about what individuals and organizations can do to reduce the threat posed by invasives.

NOTES

CHAPTER 1: THE TOAD'S TALE

1. C. Linnaeus, *Systema Naturae. Tomus 1. Editio Decima, Reformata. Laurentii Salvii, Holmiae* (1758); translation from p. 194.

2. F. C. Waite, "*Bufo agua* in the Bermudas," *Science* 13, no. 322 (1901): 342–343.

3. Quoted in J. F. Illingworth and A. P. Dodd, *Australian Sugar Cane Beetles and Their Allies* (Queensland Government, 1921).

4. James Chataway, *The Louisiana Planter and Sugar Manufacturer* 24, no. 14 (April 7, 1900).

5. G. N. Wolcott, "The White Grub Problem in Puerto Rico," *Proceedings of the Fifth Congress of International Sugar Cane Technologists* (Brisbane, 1935), pp. 445–456.

6. G. N. Wolcott, "The Rise and Fall of the White Grub in Puerto Rico," *The American Naturalist* 84 (1950): 183–193.

7. Raquel R. Dexter, "The Food Habits of the Imported Toad *Bufo marinus* in the Sugar Cane Sections of Porto Rico," *Proceedings of the Fourth Congress of International Sugar Cane Technologists*, San Juan, Puerto Rico, Bulletin 74 (1932), pp. 1–6.

8. Ibid.

9. Memo from R. W. Mungomery to A. Bell, April 19, 1935 (BSES File 507–0000 1933–1941 Introduction).

10. David Jenkins, Research Entomologist USDA-ARS Tropical Agriculture Research Station, Mayaguez, 2007; personal communication.

11. Memo from R. W. Mungomery to A. Bell, September 28, 1933 (BSES File 507–0000 1933–1941 Introduction).

12. R. W. Mungomery, "A Review of Sugar Cane Entomological Investigations," in Bureau of Sugar Experiment Stations, *Fifty Years of Scientific Progress* (Government Printer, Brisbane, 1950), pp. 38–48.

13. L. E. Caltagirone and R. L. Doutt, "The History of the Vedalia Beetle Importation to California and Its Impact on the Development of Biological Control," *Annual Review of Entomology* 34 (1989): 1–16.

14. E. Rolls, *They All Ran Wild* (Sydney: Angus and Robertson, 1969).

15. H. W. Kerr, *Thirty-Fourth Annual Report of the Bureau of Sugar Experiment Stations* (December 1934), p. 62.

16. Memo from R. W. Mungomery to A. Bell, January 10, 1935 (BSES File 507–0000 1933–1941 Introduction).

17. Memo from Director of BSES to Director-General of Health, March 25, 1935 (BSES File 507–0000 1933–1941 Introduction).

18. M. E. Nairn, P. G. Allen, A. R. Inglis, and C. Tanner, *Australian Quarantine: A Shared Responsibility* (Department of Primary Industry Canberra, 1996), p. 288.

19. Release notes in BSES File 507–000 1935–1950 Distribution.

20. *Proceedings of the International Society of Sugar Cane Technologists Fifth Congress*, Brisbane, August 27 to September 3, 1935, published by the Executive Committee.

21. W. Froggatt, "The Introduction of the Giant American Toad, *Bufo marinus*, into Australia," *The Australian Naturalist* 9, part 7 (January 1936).

22. Memo from J. Rivett to H. W. Kerr, November 18, 1935 (BSES File 507–0000 Distribution 1935–1950).

23. H. W. Kerr to R. W. Mungomery, November 12, 1935 (BSES File 507–0000 Distribution 1935–1950).

24. Memo from W. H. Doherty to H. W. Kerr, November 25, 1935 (BSES File 507–0000 Distribution 1935–1950).

25. Memo from Secretary for Agriculture and Stock to Premier of Queensland, November 22, 1935 (Queensland State Archives item ID 863194 [PRE/A1134], general correspondence 07490 of December 23, 1935).

26. B. J. Costar, "Smith, William Forgan (1887–1953)," *Australian Dictionary of Biography*; available online at http://www.adb.online.anu.edu.au/biogs/A110685b.htm.

27. Memo from Premier of Queensland to Prime Minister of the Commonwealth, December 2, 1935 (Queensland State Archives item ID 863194 [PRE/A1134], general correspondence 07490 of December 23, 1935).

28. Memo from Prime Minister to Premier of Queensland, December 17, 1935 (Queensland State Archives item ID 863194 [PRE/A1134], general correspondence 07490 of December 23, 1935.

29. Memo from J.H.L. Cumpston to Under-Secretary Department of Agriculture, Brisbane, December 4, 1935 (BSES File 507–0000 Distribution 1935–1950).

30. Froggatt, "The Introduction of the Giant American Toad, *Bufo marinus*, into Australia."

31. Memo from W. W. Froggatt to A. Bell, April 1936 (BSES File 507–0000 Distribution 1935–1950).

32. Froggatt, "The Introduction of the Giant American Toad, *Bufo marinus*, into Australia."

33. Memo from W. W. Froggatt to A. Bell, April 1936 (BSES File 507–0000 Distribution 1935–1950).

34. Memo from C. E. Pemberton to A. Bell, May 11, 1936 (BSES File 507–0000 Distribution 1935–1950).

35. Memo from Assistant Director to Director-General of Health, August 31, 1936 (BSES File 507–0000 Distribution 1935–1950).

36. Memo from Assistant Director to R. W. Mungomery, September 21, 1936 (BSES File 507–0000 Distribution 1935–1950).

37. A. J. Gibson, presidential address, in *Fifth Congress of International Sugar Cane Technologists* (Brisbane, 1935), p. 35.

38. Anonymous, *The Australian Cane Sugar Industry* (Sugar Industry Organisations, 1936).

39. H. W. Kerr and A. F. Bell, *The Queensland Cane Growers' Handbook* (Bureau of Sugar Experiment Stations. Department of Agriculture, Brisbane, 1939), p. 172.

40. P. B. Medawar, *The Art of the Soluble* (Pelican Books, 1969), pp. 142, 148.

CHAPTER 3: THE ROGUE SPECIES THREAT

1. Millennium Ecosystem Assessment, *Synthesis Report* (Kuala Lumpur, Malaysia, 2005); available online at www.maweb.org.

2. Gregory Ruiz et al., "Global Spread of Micro-Organisms by Ships," *Nature* 408 (2000): 49–50.

3. Robert H. Boyle, "Flying Fever," *Audubon* (July–August 2000): 63–68.

4. Deborah McKenzie, "Plague on a National Icon," *New Scientist* 26 (October 2002): 14–15.

5. Peter Daszak, A. Cunningham, and A. D. Hyatt, "Emerging Infectious Diseases of Wildlife: Threats to Biodiversity and Human Health," *Science* 287 (2000): 443–449.

6. Joseph P. Dudley and Michael H. Woodford, "Bioweapons, Biodiversity, and Ecocide: Potential Effects of Biological Weapons on Biological Diversity," *BioScience* 52, no. 7 (2002): 583–592.

7. Daszak, Cunningham, and Hyatt, "Emerging Infectious Diseases of Wildlife."

8. Christy Campbell, *The Botanist and the Vintner: How Wine Was Saved for the World* (Chapel Hill, NC: Algonquin Books, 2005).

9. Brian Leung, D. M. Lodge, D. Finnoff, J. Shogren, M. Lewis, and G. Lamberti, "An Ounce of Prevention or a Pound of Cure: Bioeconomic Risk Analysis of Invasive Species," *Proceedings of the Royal Society B: Biological Sciences* 269 (2002): 2407–2413.

10. Liba Pejchar and Harold A. Mooney, "Invasive Species, Ecosystem Services and Human Well-Being," *Trends in Ecology and Evolution* 24, no. 9 (2009): 497–504.

11. D. C. Le Maitre, D. B. Versfeld, and R. A. Chapman, "The Impact of Invading Alien Plants on Surface Water Resources in South Africa: A Preliminary Assessment," *Water SA* 26, no. 3 (2000): 397–407.

12. D. Pimentel, L. Lach, R. Zuniga, and D. Morrison, "Environmental and Economic Costs of Non-Indigenous Species in the United States," *BioScience* 50 (2000): 53–65.

13. Peter Aldhous, "The Toads Are Coming!" *Nature* 432 (2004): 796–798.

14. Stephanie Payne, "Farmer Buckley's Exploding Trousers," *New Scientist* 11 (December 2004): 48–49.

15. Richard Blaustein, "Kudzu's Invasion into Southern Life and Culture," in J. A. McNeely, ed., *The Great Reshuffling: Human Dimensions of Invasive Alien Species* (Gland, Switzerland: World Conservation Union, 2001), pp. 55–62.

16. K. R. McKaye et al., "African Tilapia in Lake Nicaragua," *BioScience* 45, no. 6 (1995): 406–411.

17. Pimentel et al., "Environmental and Economic Costs of Non-Indigenous Species in the United States."

18. John J. Ewel et al., "Deliberate Introductions of Species: Research Needs," *BioScience* 49, no. 8 (1999): 619–630.

19. Roland A. Knapp, "Effects of Non-Native Fish and Habitat Characteristics on Lintic Herpetofauna in Yosemite National Park, USA," *Biological Conservation* 121 (2004): 265–279.

20. Pimentel et al., "Environmental and Economic Costs of Non-Indigenous Species in the United States."

21. J.-Y. Meyer, "Tahiti's Native Flora Endangered by the Invasion of *Miconia calvescens*," *Journal of Geography* 23 (1997): 775–781.

22. T. M. Blackburn, P. Cassey, R. T. Duncan, K. L. Evans, and K. J. Gaston, "Avian Extinction and Mammalian Introductions on Oceanic Islands," *Science* 305 (2004): 1955–1958.

23. D. A. Croll, J. L. Maron, J. A. Estes, E. M. Danner, and G. V. Byrd, "Introduced Predators Transform Sub-Arctic Islands from Grassland to Tundra," *Science* 307 (2005): 1959–1961.

24. Pimentel et al., "Environmental and Economic Costs of Non-Indigenous Species in the United States."

25. Yan Xie, "Invasive Species in China: An Overview," paper prepared for the Biodiversity Working Group of the China Council for International Cooperation on Environment and Development, Beijing, 1999.

26. Haigen Xu et al., "The Status and Causes of Alien Species Invasion in China," *Biodiversity and Conservation* 15 (2006): 2893–2904.

27. Dennis Normile, "Expanding Trade with China Creates Ecological Backlash," *Science* 306 (2004): 968–969.

28. M. R. Orr and T. B. Smith, "Ecology and Speciation," *Trends in Evolution and Ecology* 13, no. 12 (1998): 503–506.

29. A. D. Kendall and J. E. Rose. "The Aliens Have Landed! What Are the Justifications for 'Native Only' Policies in Landscape Plantings?" *Landscape and Urban Planning* 47 (2000): 19–31.

CHAPTER 4: DANGEROUS STRANGERS

1. J. Moody, "Secretary Kempthorne, Secretary Schafer and Other Leaders Adopt National Plan to Combat Invasive Species," Press Release, U.S. Department of the Interior, Washington, DC, 2008.

2. Report of the Invasive Species Specialists Group; available online at http://www.issg.org/.

3. G. Rodda, R. Reed, and S. Snow, "USGS Maps Show Potential Non-Native Python Habitat Along Three U.S. Coasts," U.S. Department of the Interior, U.S. Geological Survey, 2008; available online at http://www.usgs.gov/newsroom/article.asp?ID=1875.

4. University of Florida, "Invasion of Gigantic Burmese Pythons in South Florida Appears to Be Rapidly Expanding," *ScienceDaily*, May 22, 2008; available online at http://www.sciencedaily.com/releases/2008/05/080520131750.htm.

5. R. G. Harvey, M. L. Brien, M. S. Cherkiss, M. Dorcas, M. Rochford, and R. W. Snow et al., "Burmese Pythons in South Florida: Scientific Support for Invasive Species Management," WEC242, University of Florida IFAS Extension, 2008; available online at http://edis.ifas.ufl.edu/uw286.

6. Associated Press, "South Florida Hunt for Burmese Python Ends," *Sun Sentinel* (Fort Lauderdale), November 4, 2009.

7. R. N. Reed and G. H. Rodda, "Giant Constrictors: Biological and Management Profiles and an Establishment Risk Assessment for Nine Large Species of Pythons, Anacondas, and the Boa Constrictor," U.S. Geological Survey Open-File Report 2009–1202.

8. Ibid.

9. J. K. Wetterer, L.D. Wood, C. Johnson, H. Krahe, and S. Fitchett, "Predaceous Ants, Beach Replenishment, and Nest Placement by Sea Turtles," *Environmental Entomology* 36, no. 5 (2007): 1084–1091.

10. K. M. Jetter, J. Hamilton, and J. H. Klotz, "Eradication Costs Calculated . . . Red Imported Fire Ants Threaten Agriculture, Wildlife and Homes," *California Agriculture* 56, no. 1 (2002): 26–34.

11. American Bird Conservancy, "Mortality Threat to Birds—Red Fire Ant (*Solenopsis invicta*)," 2007; available online at http://www.abcbirds.org/conservationissues/threats/invasives/ants.html.

12. M. A. Seymour, "Effect of Red Imported Fire Ant (*Solenopsis invicta buren*) on the Nesting Success of Northern Bobwhite (*Colinus virginianus l.*)," Master's thesis, Louisiana State University.

13. Ibid.

14. Audubon, "Cooling the Hot Spots Protecting America's Birds, Wildlife, and Natural Heritage from Invasive Species," Washington, DC, n.d.; available online at http://www.stopinvasives.org/pdf/invasives_report_2nd_edition.pdf; Seymour, "Effect of Red Imported Fire Ant (*Solenopsis invicta buren*) on the Nesting Success of Northern Bobwhite (*Colinus virginianus l.*)." See also A. J. Campomizzi, M. L. Morrison, S. L. Farrell, R. N. Wilkins, B. M. Drees, and J. M. Packard, "Red Imported Fire Ants Can Decrease Songbird Nest Survival," *The Condor* 111, no. 3 (2009): 534–537.

15. Wetterer et al., "Predaceous Ants, Beach Replenishment, and Nest Placement by Sea Turtles."

16. "Frequently Asked Questions About the Zebra Mussel," United States Geological Survey, United States Department of the Interior, 2009; available online at http://fl.biology.usgs.gov/Nonindigenous_Species/Zebra_mussel_FAQs/zebra_mussel_faqs.html.

17. J. D. Williams, N. Melvin, J. Warren, K. S. Cummings, J. L. Harris, and R. J. Neves, "Conservation Status of Freshwater Mussels of the United States and Canada," *Fisheries* 18, no. 9 (September 1993).

18. Associated Press, "Federal Officials Unveil Blueprint for Great Lakes," *New York Times*, February 22, 2010, p. A11.

19. A. Ricciardi, "Assessing Species Invasions as a Cause of Extinction," *Trends in Ecology and Evolution* 19, no. 12 (2004): 619.

20. C. Dell'Amore, "Hybrid 'Superpredator' Invading California Ponds," *National Geographic News*; available online at http://news.nationalgeographic.com/news/2009/06/090629-salamanders-hybrid.html. See also M. E. Ryan, J. R. Johnson, and B. M. Fitzpatrick, "Invasive Hybrid Tiger Salamander Genotypes Impact Native

Amphibians," *Proceedings of the National Academy of Sciences of the United States of America* 106, no. 27 (2009): 11166–11171.

21. ScienceMode, "California Barred Tiger Salamanders Interbreed Produce Hybrids," 2007; available online at http://sciencemode.com/2007/09/20/california-barred-tiger-salamanders-interbreed-produce-hybrids/.

22. Ryan, Johnson, and Fitzpatrick, "Invasive Hybrid Tiger Salamander Genotypes Impact Native Amphibians."

23. Dell'Amore, "Hybrid 'Superpredator' Invading California Ponds"; Ryan, Johnson, and Fitzpatrick, "Invasive Hybrid Tiger Salamander Genotypes Impact Native Amphibians."

24. ScienceMode, "California Barred Tiger Salamanders Interbreed Produce Hybrids."

25. I. R. Ragenovich and R. G. Mitchell, "Forest Insect & Disease Leaflet 118: Balsam Woolly Adelgid" (U.S. Department of Agriculture, Forest Service, 2006), p. 12.

26. David N. Wear and John G. Greis, eds., "Southern Forest Resource Assessment," Gen. Tech. Rep. SRS-53 (Asheville, NC: U.S. Department of Agriculture, Forest Service, Southern Research Station, 2002), p. 635. See also K. M. Potter, J. Frampton, and J. Sidebottom, "Impacts of Balsam Woolly Adelgid on the Southern Appalachian Spruce-Fir Ecosystem and the North Carolina Christmas Tree Industry," in *Third Symposium on Hemlock Woolly Adelgid in the Eastern United States* (Asheville, NC: USDA Forest Service, 2005), p. 17.

27. Ragenovich and Mitchell, "Forest Insect & Disease Leaflet 118: Balsam Woolly Adelgid."

28. Wear and Greis, "Southern Forest Resource Assessment."

29. D. P. Reinhart, M. A. Haroldson, D. J. Mattson, and K. A. Gunther, "Effects of Exotic Species on Yellowstone's Grizzly Bears," *Western North American Naturalist* 61, no. 3 (2001): 277–288.

30. Ibid.

31. D. Simberloff, "Global Climate Change and Introduced Species in United States Forests," *The Science of the Total Environment* 262 (2000): 253–261.

32. Buffelgrass Information Center, "History & Distribution, Arizona-Sonora Desert Museum"; available online at http://www.buffelgrass.org/index.php.

33. J. S. Dukes and H. A. Mooney, "Does Global Change Increase the Success of Biological Invaders? *Tree* 14, no. 4 (1999): 135–139.

34. RedOrbit News, "Pygmy Owl May Be Endangered Species"; available online at http://www.redorbit.com/modules/news/tools.php?tool=print&id=1410764.

35. M. L. Brooks, T. C. Esque, and C. R. Schalbe, "Effects of Exotic Grasses via Wildfire on Desert Tortoises and Their Habitat," *Twenty-Fourth Annual Meeting and Symposium of the Desert Tortoise Council*, March 5–8, 1999.

36. "The Tamarisk Invasion: White Sands National Monument," 2004; available online at http://www.nps.gov/archive/whsa/tamarisk.htm.

37. T. A. Kennedy, J. C. Finlay, and S. E. Hobbie, "Eradication of Invasive *Tamarix ramosissima* Along a Desert Stream Increases Native Fish Density," *Ecological Applications* 15, no. 6 (2005): 2072–2083.

38. "The Tamarisk Invasion: White Sands National Monument," 2004; available online at http://www.nps.gov/archive/whsa/tamarisk.htm.

39. Kennedy, Finlay, and Hobbie, "Eradication of Invasive *Tamarix ramosissima* Along a Desert Stream Increases Native Fish Density"; T. A. Kennedy and S. E. Hobbie, "Saltcedar (*Tamarix ramosissima*) Invasion Alters Organic Matter Dynamics in a Desert Stream," *Freshwater Biology* 49 (2004): 65–76. See also K. D. Lair, "Revegetation Strategies and Technologies for Restoration of Aridic Saltcedar (*Tamarix spp.*)," Infestation Sites, RMRS-P-43, USDA Forest Service Proceedings, 2006.

40. The Nature Conservancy, "Invasive Species: What You Can Do, Bad Plants in Your Backyard: Purple Loosestrife," 2008; available online at http://www.nature.org/initiatives/invasivespecies/features/art8863.html.

41. D. Q. Thompson, R. L. Stuckey, and E. B. Thompson, "Spread, Impact, and Control of Purple Loosestrife (*Lythrum salicaria*) in North American Wetlands," 2006; available online at http://www.npwrc.usgs.gov/resource/plants/loosstrf/index.htm.

42. J. M. Swearingen, "Fact Sheet: Purple Loosestrife" (Plant Conservation Alliance Alien Plant Working Group, 2005), p. 3; available online at http://www.nps.gov/plants/alien/.

43. E. T. Smith, "Bog Turtle (*Clemmys muhlenbergii*)," edited by National Resources Conservation Service (Washington, DC: Fish and Wildlife Management Leaflet, 2006).

44. Thompson, Stuckey, and Thompson, "Spread, Impact, and Control of Purple Loosestrife (*Lythrum salicaria*) in North American Wetlands"; B. L. Sanderson, K. A. Barnas, and M. W. Rub, "Nonindigenous Species of the Pacific Northwest: An Overlooked Risk to Endangered Salmon," *BioScience* 59, no. 3 (2009): 245–256.

45. Sanderson, Barnas, and Rub, "Nonindigenous Species of the Pacific Northwest: An Overlooked Risk to Endangered Salmon."

46. Audubon, "Cooling the Hot Spots: Protecting America's Birds, Wildlife, and Natural Heritage from Invasive Species."

47. Ibid.

Chapter 6: Hawaii: Paradise Lost

1. D. R. Sherrod, "Hawaiian Islands, Geology," in R. G. Gillespie and D. A. Clague, eds., *Encyclopedia of Islands* (pp. 404–410) (Berkeley: University of California Press, 2009).

2. B. G. Baldwin, "Silverswords," in R. G. Gillespie and D. A. Clague, eds., *Encyclopedia of Islands* (pp. 835–839) (Berkeley: University of California Press, 2009).

3. P. M. O'Grady, K. N. Magnacca, and R.T. Lapointe, "Drosophila," in R. G. Gillespie and D. A. Clague, eds., *Encyclopedia of Islands* (pp. 232–235) (Berkeley: University of California Press, 2009).

4. R. H. Cowie, "Pacific Island Land Snails: Relationships, Origins and Determinants of Diversity," in A. Keast and S. E. Miller, eds., *The Origin and Evolution of Pacific Island Biotas, New Guinea to Eastern Polynesia: Patterns and Processes* (pp. 347–372) (Amsterdam: SPB Academic, 1996); B. S. Holland, "Land Snails," in R. G. Gillespie and D. A. Clague, eds., *Encyclopedia of Islands* (pp. 537–542) (Berkeley: University of California Press, 2009).

5. A. J. Berger, *Hawaiian Birds*, 2nd ed. (Honolulu: University of Hawaii Press, 1981).

6. R. C. Fleischer, "Honeycreepers, Hawaiian," in R. G. Gillespie and D. A. Clague, eds., *Encyclopedia of Islands* (pp. 410–414) (Berkeley: University of California Press, 2009).

7. P. V. Kirch, "The Impact of Prehistoric Polynesians on the Hawaiian Ecosystem," *Pacific Science* 36 (1982): 1–14; P. V. Kirch, "Transported Landscapes," *Natural History* 91, no. 12 (1982): 32–35.

8. J. S. Athens, *Rattus exulans* and the Catastrophic Disappearance of Hawai'i's Native Lowland Forest," *Biological Invasions* 11 (2009): 1489–1501.

9. S. L. Olson and H. F. James, "Fossil Birds from the Hawaiian Islands: Evidence for Wholesale Extinction by Man Before Western Contact," *Science* 217 (1982): 633–635.

10. C. van Riper III, S. van Riper, M. L. Goff, and M. Laird, "The Epizootiology and Ecological Significance of Malaria in Hawaiian Land Birds," *Ecological Monographs* 56 (1986): 327–344; F. G. Howarth, G. M. Nishida, and N. J. Evenhuis, "Insects and Other Terrestrial Arthropods," in G.W. Staples and R. H. Cowie, eds., *Hawai'i's Invasive Species* (pp. 41–62) (Honolulu: Mutual Publishing, 2001).

11. P. R. Ehrlich, D. S. Dobkin, and D. Wheye, *Birds in Jeopardy* (Stanford, CA: Stanford University Press, 1992).

12. B. L. Woodworth, C.T. Atkinson, D. A. LaPointe, P. J. Hart, C. S. Spiegel, E. J. Tweed, C. Henneman, J. LeBrun, T. Denette, R. DeMots, K. L. Kozar, D. Triglia, D. Lease, A. Gregor, T. Smith, and D. Duffy, "Host Population Persistence in the Face of Introduced Vector-Borne Diseases: Hawaii Amakihi and Avian Malaria," *Proceedings of the National Academy of Sciences* (U.S.) 102 (2005): 1531–1536.

13. C. Lever, *They Dined on Eland: The Story of the Acclimatisation Societies* (London: Quiller, 1992).

14. C. H. Kishinami, "Birds," in G. W. Staples and R. H. Cowie, eds., *Hawai'i's Invasive Species* (pp. 20–27) (Honolulu: Mutual Publishing, 2001).

15. C. H. Kishinami, "Mammals," in G. W. Staples and R. H. Cowie, eds., *Hawai'i's Invasive Species* (pp. 17–20) (Honolulu: Mutual Publishing, 2001); W.S.T. Hays and S. Conant, "Impact of the Small Indian Mongoose (*Herpestes javanicus*) (Carnivora: Herpestidae) on Native Vertebrate Populations in Areas of Introduction," *Pacific Science* 61 (2007): 3–16.

16. C. M. D'Antonio and P. M. Vitousek, "Biological Invasions by Exotic Grasses, the Grass/Fire Cycle, and Global Change," *Annual Review of Ecology and Systematics* 23 (1992): 63–87.

17. G. P. Asner and P. M. Vitousek, "Remote Analysis of Biological Invasion and Biogeochemical Change," *Proceedings of the National Academy of Sciences* (U.S.) 102 (2005): 4383–4386.

18. G. H. Aplet, "Alteration of Earthworm Community Biomass by the Alien *Myrica faya* in Hawai'i," *Oecologia* 82 (1990): 414–416.

19. G. W. Staples, "Plants," in G. W. Staples and R. H. Cowie, eds., *Hawai'i's Invasive Species* (pp. 76–99) (Honolulu: Mutual Publishing, 2001).

20. Ibid.

21. D. Simberloff, "Invasions of Plant Communities—More of the Same, or Something Very Different?" *American Midland Naturalist* 163 (2009): 219–232.

22. Howarth, Nishida, and Evenhuis, "Insects and Other Terrestrial Arthropods."

23. L. Civeyrel and D. Simberloff, "A Tale of Two Snails: Is the Cure Worse Than the Disease?" *Biodiversity and Conservation* 5 (1996): 1231–1252.

24. Anonymous, "Species Not Wanted in the Hawaiian Islands," in G. W. Staples and R. H. Cowie, eds., *Hawai'i's Invasive Species* (pp. 12–13) (Honolulu: Mutual Publishing, 2001).

25. Ibid.

26. G. W. Staples and R. H. Cowie, Introduction, in G. W. Staples and R. H. Cowie, eds., *Hawai'i's Invasive Species* (Honolulu: Mutual Publishing, 2001), pp. 1–10.

27. M. L. Miller, "Federal and State Laws," in D. Simberloff and M. Rejmánek, eds., *Encyclopedia of Biological Invasions* (Berkeley: University of California Press, in press).

28. D. Simberloff, "How Much Information on Population Biology Is Needed to Manage Introduced Species?" *Conservation Biology* 17 (2003): 83–92.

29. P. Tummons, "Waiwai Biocontrol Controversy," *Environment Hawaii* 19, no. 1 (2008).

30. F. Kraus, *Alien Reptiles and Amphibians* (Berlin: Springer, 2009).

31. Kishinami, "Mammals."

32. A. Burdick, *Out of Eden. An Odyssey of Ecological Invasion* (New York: Farrar, Straus and Giroux, 2005).

33. D. Simberloff, "We Can Eliminate Invasions or Live with Them! High-Tech and Low-Tech Success Stories," *Biological Invasions* 11 (2009): 149–157.

34. M. J. Rauzon and D. C. Drigot, "Red Mangrove Eradication and Pickleweed Control in a Hawaiian Wetland, Waterbird Responses, and Lessons Learned, in C. R. Veitch and M. N. Clout, eds., *Turning the Tide: The Eradication of Invasive Species* (pp. 240–248) (Gland, Switzerland: IUCN SSC Invasive Species Specialist Group, 2002).

35. E. Flint and C. Rehkemper, "Control and Eradication of the Introduced Grass, *Cenchrus echinatus*, at Laysan Island, Central Pacific Ocean," in C. R. Veitch and M. N. Clout, eds., *Turning the Tide: The Eradication of Invasive Species* (Gland, Switzerland: IUCN SSC Invasive Species Specialist Group, 2002).

CHAPTER 8: WILDLIFE TRADE AND INVASIVE SPECIES

1. C. R. Shepherd, E. A. Burgess, and M. Loo, *Demand Driven: The Trade of Indian Star Tortoises* Geochelone elegans *in Peninsular Malaysia* (TRAFFIC Southeast Asia, 2004); G. L. Warchol, "The Transnational Illegal Wildlife Trade," *Criminal Justice Studies* 17, no. 1 (2004): 57–73.

2. TRAFFIC, "What's Driving the Wildlife Trade? A Review of Expert Opinion on Economic and Social Drivers of the Wildlife Trade and Trade Control Efforts in Cambodia, Indonesia, Lao PDR and Vietnam," East Asia and Pacific Region sustainable development discussion papers (East Asia and the Pacific Region Sustainable Development Department, World Bank, Washington, DC, 2008).

3. C. R. Shepherd and B. Ibarrondo, *The Trade of the Roti Island Snake-Necked Turtle* Chelodina mccordi, *Indonesia* (TRAFFIC Southeast Asia, 2005); F. Courchamp,

E. Angulo, P. Rivalan, R. J. Hall, L. Signoret, L. Bull, and Y. Meinard, "Rarity Value and Species Extinction: The Anthropogentic Effect," *PLoS Biology* 4, no. 12 (2006).

4. V. Nijman, C. R. Shepherd, and S. van Balen, "Declaration of the Javan Hawk-Eagle *Spizaetus bartelsi* as Indonesia's National Rare Animal Impedes Conservation of the Species," *Oryx* 43, no. 1 (2009): 122–128.

5. V. Nijman and C. R. Shepherd, "Trade in Non-Native, CITES-Listed Wildlife in Asia, as Exemplified by the Trade in Freshwater Turtles and Tortoises (Chelonidae) in Thailand," *Contributions to Zoology* 76, no. 3 (2007): 207–212.

6. C. R. Shepherd and V. Nijman, *The Wild Cat Trade in Myanmar* (TRAFFIC Southeast Asia, Petaling Jaya, Malaysia, 2008).

7. C. R. Shepherd and L. A. Shepherd, "An Emerging Asian Taste for Owls? Enforcement Agency Seizes 1,236 Owls and Other Wildlife in Malaysia," *Birding ASIA* 11 (2009): 85–86.

8. C. R. Shepherd, "Export of Live Freshwater Turtles and Tortoises from North Sumatra and Riau, Indonesia: A Case Study," in P. P. van Dijk, B. L. Stuart, and A.G.J. Rhodin, eds., *Asian Turtle Trade: Proceedings of a Workshop on Conservation and Trade of Freshwater Turtles and Tortoises in Asia*, Chelonian Research Monographs, No. 2 (2000).

9. N. Baker and K. Lim, *Wild Animals of Singapore* (Singapore: Draco Publishing and Distribution and Nature Society, 2008).

10. R. T. Corlett, *The Ecology of Tropical East Asia* (New York: Oxford University Press, 2009).

11. Shepherd, Burgess, and Loo, *Demand Driven*.

12. N. Baker and K. Lim, *Wild Animals of Singapore* (Singapore: Draco Publishing and Distribution and Nature Society, 2008).

13. P. P. Van Dijk, B. L. Stuart, and A.G.L. Rhodin, eds., *Asian Turtle Trade: Proceedings of a Workshop on Conservation and Trade of Freshwater Turtles and Tortoises in Asia*, Chelonian Research Monographs, No. 2 (2000).

14. L. M. Close and R. A. Seigel, "Differences in Body Size Among Populations of Red-Eared Sliders (*Trachemys scripta elegans*) Subjected to Different Levels of Harvesting," *Chelonian Conservation and Biology* 2, no. 4 (1997): 563–566.

15. D. Senneke, "Declared Turtle Trade From the United States," World Chelonian Trust (2006); available online at www.chelonia.org/articles/us/usmarketintropage.htm.

16. C. H. Ernst, J. E. Lovich, and R. W. Barbour, *Turtles of the United States and Canada* (Washington, DC: Smithsonian Institution Press, 2009).

17. "Issues—Results of the Turtle Trade–Feral Population Threats," World Chelonian Trust (2006); available online at http://www.chelonia.org/articles/us/Feral_issues.htm.

18. Species were selected for the list according to two criteria: their serious impact on biological diversity and/or human activities, and their illustration of important issues surrounding biological invasion. To ensure the inclusion of a wide variety of examples, only one species from each genus was selected.

19. G. Semiadi, D. Darnaedi, and J. Arief, "Sunda Pangolin *Manis javanica* Conservation in Indonesia: Status and Problems," in S. Pantel and S. Y. Chin, eds., *Proceedings of the Workshop on Trade and Conservation of Pangolins Native to South and Southeast Asia, 30 June–2 July 2008* (TRAFFIC Southeast Asia, Selangor, Malaysia, 2009).

20. S. Wu, N. Liu, Y. Zhang, and G. Ma, "Assessment of Threatened Status of Chinese Pangolin (*Manis pentadactyla*)," *Chinese Journal of Applied Environmental Biology* 10, no. 4 (2004): 456–461; and C. Liou, ed., *The State of Wildlife Trade in China: Information on the Trade in Wild Animals and Plants in China 2006* (TRAFFIC East Asia, China, 2006).

21. H. Li and H. Wang, "Wildlife Trade in Yunnan Province, China, at the Border with Vietnam," *TRAFFIC Bulletin* 18, no. 1 (2008): 21–30.

22. S. Kang and M. Phipps, *A Question of Attitude: South Korea's Traditional Medicine Practitioners and Wildlife Conservation* (TRAFFIC East Asia, Hong Kong, 2003).

23. L. Clark, V. T. Nguyen, and Q. P. Tran, *A Long Way from Home: The Health Status of Asian Pangolins Confiscated from the Illegal Wildlife Trade in Viet Nam,* in S. Pantel and S. Y. Chin, eds., *Proceedings of the Workshop on Trade and Conservation of Pangolins Native to South and Southeast Asia, 30 June–2 July 2008* (TRAFFIC Southeast Asia, Selangor, Malaysia, 2009); N. Heng and A. Olsson, *Pangolin Research in Cambodia,* in S. Pantel and S. Y. Chin, eds., *Proceedings of the Workshop on Trade and Conservation of Pangolins Native to South and Southeast Asia, 30 June–2 July 2008* (TRAFFIC Southeast Asia, Selangor, Malaysia, 2009).

24. Clark, Nguyen, and Tran, *A Long Way from Home.*

25. Ibid.

26. International Union for the Conservation of Nature, "IUCN Red List of Threatened Species," Version 2009.1; available online at www.iucnredlist.org (downloaded on October 10, 2009).

27. N. Pallewatta, J. K. Reaser, and A. T. Gutierrez, eds., "Invasive Alien Species in South-Southeast Asia: National Reports and Directory of Resources" (Global Invasive Species Programme, Cape Town, South Africa, 2002).

Chapter 11: Government Policy and the Rogue Species Crisis

1. D. Pimentel, R. Zuniga, and D. Morrison, "Update on the Environmental and Economic Costs Associated with Alien-Invasive Species in the United States," *Ecological Economics* 52 (2005): 273–288; digital object identifier (DOI): 10.1016/j.ecolecon.2004.07.013.

2. K. F. Kovacs et al., "Cost of Potential Emerald Ash Borer Damage in U.S. Communities, 2009–2019," *Ecological Economics* 68 (2009); DOI: 10.1016/j.ecolecon.2009.09.004.

3. F. J. Rahel and J. D. Olden, "Assessing the Effects of Climate Change on Aquatic Invasive Species," *Conservation Biology* 22, no. 3 (2008): 521–533.

4. J. S. Dukes and H. A. Mooney, "Does Global Change Increase the Success of Biological Invaders?" *Tree* 14, no. 4 (April 1999).

5. P. T. Jenkins, K. Genovese, and H. Ruffler, "Broken Screens: The Regulation of Live Animal Imports in the United States" (Washington, DC, Defenders of Wildlife, 2007).

6. A. J. Fowler, D. M. Lodge, and J. F. Hsia, "Failure of the Lacey Act to Protect U.S. Ecosystems Against Animal Invasions," *Frontiers in Ecology and the Environment* 5, no. 7 (2007): 353–359.

7. Title I of P.L. 101–646; 16 U.S.C. §§4701, et seq.

8. Eugene H. Buck, "Ballast Water Management to Combat Invasive Species," Congressional Research Service, 7–5700, RI32344 (April 16, 2009); available online at www.crs.gov.

9. *Federal Register* 64, nos. 26672–26690 (May 17, 1999). These voluntary guideline

regulations were effective as of July 1, 1999.

10. If the voluntary program did not result in sufficient compliance, reporting of BWM practices would become mandatory for nearly all vessels entering U.S. waters (33 CFR 151.2040).

11. G. M. Ruiz et al., *Status and Trends of Ballast Water Management in the United States: First Biennial Report of the National Ballast Information Clearinghouse* (Edgewater, MD: Smithsonian Environmental Research Center, November 16, 2001), p. 4.

12. U.S. Coast Guard, *Report to Congress on the Effectiveness of the Voluntary BWM Program*, June 3, 2002.

13. *Federal Register* 68, nos. 523–530 (January 6, 2003).

14. Letter of February 11, 1999, to Hon. Carol Browner, administrator of the U.S. Environmental Protection Agency, from Representatives George Miller, Jim Saxton, and sixteen other members of the U.S. House of Representatives.

15. Union of Concerned Scientists, "The National Invasive Species Act: An Information Update" (Cambridge, MA, August 2002); available online at http://www.ucsusa.org/assets/documents/invasive_species/nisa-1.pdf.

16. Jenkins, Genovese, and Ruffler, "Broken Screens: The Regulation of Live Animal Imports in the United States."

17. Phyllis Windle, Union of Concerned Scientist, "The Facts vs. the Myths: Why We Need H.R. 669 To Prevent Invasive Species"; available online at http://www.ucsusa.org/invasive_species/solutions/hr669-facts.html.

18. State Water Resources Control Board, *Evaluation of Ballast Water Treatment Technology for Control of Nonindigenous Aquatic Organisms*, California Environmental Protection Agency (December 2002); available online at http://www.calepa.ca.gov/Publications/Reports/Mandated/2002/BallastWater.pdf.

19. Frans J. Tjallingii, *Market Opportunities for Ballast Water Treatment*, Royal Haskoning, International Ballast Technology Investment Fair, Chicago, September 21, 2001; available online at http://www.nemw.org/fairtjallingii.pdf.

20. As of July 2003, U.S. flag vessels comprised 1.65 percent of the global merchant fleet tonnage, according to statistics from the U.S. Maritime Administration; available online at http://www.marad.dot.gov/Marad_Statistics/mfw-7–03.htm.

INDEX

I believe that a good story well told can truly make a difference in how one sees the world. This is why I started Participant Media: to tell compelling, entertaining stories that create awareness of the real issues that shape our lives.

At Participant, we seek to entertain our audiences first, and then invite them to participate in making a difference. With each film, we create social action and advocacy programs that highlight the issues that resonate in the film and provide ways to transform the impact of the media experience into individual and community action.

Twenty-five films later, from GOOD NIGHT, AND GOOD LUCK to AN INCONVENIENT TRUTH, and from FOOD, INC. to FURRY VENGEANCE and OCEANS, and through thousands of social action activities, Participant continues to create entertainment that inspires and compels social change. Now through our partnership with PublicAffairs, we are extending our mission so that more of you can join us in making our world a better place.

Jeff Skoll, Founder and Chairman
Participant Media

PublicAffairs is a publishing house founded in 1997. It is a tribute to the standards, values, and flair of three persons who have served as mentors to countless reporters, writers, editors, and book people of all kinds, including me.

I. F. STONE, proprietor of *I. F. Stone's Weekly*, combined a commitment to the First Amendment with entrepreneurial zeal and reporting skill and became one of the great independent journalists in American history. At the age of eighty, Izzy published *The Trial of Socrates*, which was a national bestseller. He wrote the book after he taught himself ancient Greek.

BENJAMIN C. BRADLEE was for nearly thirty years the charismatic editorial leader of *The Washington Post*. It was Ben who gave the *Post* the range and courage to pursue such historic issues as Watergate. He supported his reporters with a tenacity that made them fearless and it is no accident that so many became authors of influential, best-selling books.

ROBERT L. BERNSTEIN, the chief executive of Random House for more than a quarter century, guided one of the nation's premier publishing houses. Bob was personally responsible for many books of political dissent and argument that challenged tyranny around the globe. He is also the founder and longtime chair of Human Rights Watch, one of the most respected human rights organizations in the world.

• • •

For fifty years, the banner of Public Affairs Press was carried by its owner Morris B. Schnapper, who published Gandhi, Nasser, Toynbee, Truman, and about 1,500 other authors. In 1983, Schnapper was described by *The Washington Post* as "a redoubtable gadfly." His legacy will endure in the books to come.

Peter Osnos, *Founder and Editor-at-Large*